*'Continuing The Journey'*

2

# THE ROYAL SAILOR STAGECOACH

## 1811 - 1842

## THE ROUTE FROM CARLISLE TO WHITEHAVEN

**By SHIRLEY L. THORNHILL**

*Shirley L. Thornhill*

**Colour Photographs by the Author &
Margaret Sharp
Pen & Wash Drawings by the Author**

First published December 2008
By Shirley L. Thornhill
9 Longthwaite Crescent
Wigton
Cumbria
CA7 9JN

ISBN No. 978-0-9561157-0-6

Printed by Fingerprints, Barrow-in-Furness.

# Contents

for my sons
Gary and Mark

# ACKNOWLEDGEMENTS

I would like to thank the many people who have helped me with my researches, which enabled me to write this book. To name a few Susan Dench and the staff at the Carlisle Record Office; Whitehaven Record Office; Stephen White and his staff at the Carlisle County Library, Workington Library and Stephen Matthews of Bookcase, Carlisle.

The Beacon Museum, Mike Pritt, Keith Thompson, Trevor Grahamslaw, Ashley Kendal, Philip Cueto, Mr Wilson, David Cash, Mr D. Atkinson and Jim Templeton for copies of old photographs from their various collections.

Those that kindly proof read the script Dennis Perriam, Ralph Lewthwaite, Catherine Bottomly, Pat Coyle and Mary Canfield. Melanie Gardner of Tullie House Museum & Art Gallery, for allowing me to use an image of a William Henry Nutter water colour 'Carlisle Market Cross from English Street 1835' for the book cover.

I also thank my friends Margaret Sharp and Edna Marper who tramped many a mile taking photographs and searching the record offices with me. My thanks go to my husband for putting up with my constant conversations on toll cottages, inns, roads and stagecoaches etc. I have enjoyed the researching and the writing of this book and feel very proud that it is now in print.

I would like to add that parts of this old stagecoach route can be walked and enjoyed through some of the villages, country lanes and the Solway coast as shown in the colour section of this book and the accompanying maps.

Shirley L.Thornhill
October 2008

*Taken from 'Wandering on the old Border, Lakeland' Edmund Bogg*

**Chapter One**

**STAGECOACH DAYS IN CUMBRIA**

Imagine catching the early morning stagecoach from Carlisle to
Whitehaven back in the time of 1811. It left early in the morning,
in all weathers except the middle of winter when the snow was too
deep to travel. A team of four horses sometimes six on a main route
would be hitched up to the coach. The coachman who had to be a
strong hardy man for the job and able to face the extremes of the
weather sat on top at the front dressed in his caped greatcoat and top
hat. Beside him sat the guard who was employed by the Post Office
to guard the mail. He was often armed with a pistol or blunderbuss
and carried a long post horn to sound their approach. Passengers
did not sit on the top of the coach in the very early days of travel
as it was too precarious a position they would have ended up in the
ditch. Later coaches were designed with two seats behind the driver
and two seats situated at the back over the luggage box. Inside were

two facing wooden seats taking from four to six passengers at a squeeze, with knees practically touching. On the floor straw was put down to soak up the wet and mud. At the back of the coach was strung a luggage basket known in those days as 'the conveniency behind' this would also hold passengers. It was the cheapest seat but offered no shelter from the elements, swaying with the coach it proved a rough ride. The windows in these early coaches had no glass, but in bad weather a leather curtain was rolled down, which probably did not help much in the driving rain or the dust off the road on a hot day.

Suspension in the early coaches was by leather straps this caused a swaying motion. This was superseded by steel springs. Various types were invented but the elliptical 'Telegraph' spring was the most popular, enabling the coach body to be lower and less likely to overturn. For night travelling lamps were positioned on the near side and offside at the front of the coach just high enough to be seen over the horses' rump.

Various hazards had to be contended with. These early coaches did not have brakes, and descending hills was no mean feat for driver and horses. Careful handling of the horses kept the coach at a steady pace ascending and descending. Towards the end of the coaching period brakes such as the 'shoe or drag' were introduced, these were attached to a chain and used when the coach was stationary while passengers were boarding and alighting, and to slow the pace down on descending a hill. On very steep hills passengers were required to step down and walk. Sometimes extra pairs of horses were waiting to be harnessed up to give the needed pulling power. This was done over Shap, but it is not known if it was used on any hills on the Carlisle to Whitehaven route.

Other hazards along the road such as rocks, holes, loose animals or flooded areas and especially if a coach was travelling too fast around a bend could cause accidents. Coaches coming in opposite directions and passing along a narrow stretch of road could be a problem. If a coach became stuck in a ditch it would take another team of horses to pull it out. These mishaps would upset the timetable and consequently the coach would be late at the next stage. In the case of serious accidents and many were recorded around the country with fatal results passengers that survived would have to wait until the following day for the next stagecoach, therefore they would have to accept lodgings at the nearest hostelry, unless other means of conveyance was at hand to get them to their destinations. Coaching horses also brought problems if they were not evenly matched and did not settle down together as a team such as a new horse brought in from elsewhere which made driving difficult, they got tired towards the end of their part of the route and stumbled on the rough roads especially if the driver was behind time and anxious to get to the next stage, which all added to a very uncomfortable ride.

Although stage coaching companies tried to keep running through the winter they did cease in extreme weather as it had been known for passengers and drivers to freeze to death or get stuck in heavy snow drifts in isolated places on route. The driver and guard on the Edinburgh Royal Mail perished in a snowstorm near Tweedshaws in February 1831 in their efforts to get the mail through. They are both commended for their performance to duty on memorial tablets.

The working life of a coach horse was about three to four years. They had to be fit and strong for pulling the heavy coaches loaded with passengers and luggage. At six or seven miles an hour, they travelled roughly fifteen miles a day between towns before a change, and then had to be ready to do the return journey later the same day. Different sets of horses generally worked each stage. For example horses hitched up in Carlisle travelled to Wigton where a fresh set of horses was ready for the next stage. This first set of horses were then rested ready for the return journey from Wigton

*Waiting to Change the Horses, by kind permission of Carlisle Library*

back to Carlisle. They worked three days out of four. Horses for coach work were generally supplied by the local land owners and farmers, quite often sold as unusable for any other sort of work, but they settled down in harness. Others were bred specially for coaching and used for the fast mail services.

Coachmen drove on average about fifty miles a day, for a weekly wage of approximately a guinea paid by the coach proprietors. This wage probably enhanced by the odd tip, the delivery of a parcel or a pick up fare on a short trip between stages, this was considered the coachman's perks. The coachman and guard travelled the complete distance from Carlisle to Whitehaven and returned the next day, no doubt obtaining free or cheap lodgings for the night at the respective inns or somewhere near by where the route finished. They arose early in the morning to see that all preparation was ready for that day's journey. The coach and horses were smartly turned out in the livery colour of their owners, or in the case of a Royal Mail coach in red although this was changed in 1833 by a new General Post Office regulation announced in the Carlisle Journal. *'According to the new regulations of the General Post Office, respecting the colour of the stage coaches which in future is intended to be Blue, out of compliment to the King we suppose. A mail arrived in this city on Thursday last painted after a new fashion'.* The mail coaches were not owned by the Post Office, but by contractors who supplied the coaches and drivers and they also arranged for a change of fresh horses at the various coaching inns at designated stages along the route.

Fares were charged according to where you sat. The dearest seats were inside the coach known as 1st class and the 2nd class seats were outside on top. Not the best place to be on a wet or cold windy day. Fares were charged at roughly 3 1/2p per mile but this varied from county to county. Stagecoach fares were considered expensive in comparison to the wage of the average individual. Only the well off could afford to travel by this mode of transport. As an example it is noted that one of William Senhouse's sons of Netherhall, Maryport while at school in St.Bees travelled to Arthuret near Longtown at the cost of 18s/4d., a journey of over 62 miles. A labourer in those days earned £5 per half year. They travelled about on foot, by horse, mule, or horse and cart.

Old Roman roads and drovers routes were the only roads in the early 1700's apart from cart tracks used by the local inhabitants to get from A to B across the country. These old roads were the responsibility of the various parishes. Piles of stones were kept at the side of the road and used to repair the surface. This was done by the local labourers of each parish who were obliged to work unpaid for six days of every year. Not a very satisfactory situation as the roads deteriorated very quickly in bad weather. Coaches with narrow wheels did the most damage and left deep ruts, wagons used for transporting goods had wider wheels and did not cut into the surface so much. But generally coach travel was not an easy ride, travelling could be so rough and bumpy passengers invariably arrived at their destination feeling sick, dizzy and with severe headaches. Perhaps this is when 'smelling salts' for the ladies was invented.

 Highwaymen come to mind in these dark days. They lurked in lonely out of the way places ready to jump out and demand at the point of a pistol anything of value, ladies jewellery, gentlemen's watches, money, luggage, and the mail. Often these highwaymen were tipped off that someone of distinction would be travelling that day or night and there would be good pickings. It was noted from a letter that young Humphrey Senhouse II travelled down to Cambridge from Maryport and had not met with any '*Collectors i.e. robbers on the highway*' and had arrived safely.

As traffic increased Turnpike Trusts had to be formed so that roads could be improved and maintained. This was done in varying stages through the county. The trustees were usually the local landowners and professional people such as the Lowthers, Senhouses, Curwens and Grahams who invested money in the trusts. They could see that it was to their advantage that the better roads would mean swift distribution of their goods from the ports to inland destinations and the merchants and businessman that they dealt with were able to travel about the country to conduct their various transactions. These Turnpike Trusts were not always received with enthusiasm by the local inhabitants who had to pay the various tolls. They could not see that the monies generated improved the condition of the roads that they used. Being poorly paid and scratching a meagre living from their farms and smallholdings the tolls only added further hardship.

In 1811 some land was already enclosed around the villages and towns. But the areas between were open common, moor land and moss with only a cart track showing the way. As the enclosures progressed with the dividing up of the land there was much activity. This could be seen as the coach passed between the various villages and towns. Roads were re routed around the newly formed fields, pastures and woodland owned by the local landowners. Many labourers were seen hard at work laying out these new roads, ditching, planting hedges and building walls an ever changing landscape till the enclosures were complete.

A meeting was advertised in the Cumberland Paquet in May 1811 regarding lands in the townships of *'Wigton, Woodside and Waverton within the Barony of Wigton to be held at the house of Richard Rigg, Innholder at Wigton by the appointed Commissioners John Nicholson, John Norman, and Ric*hard *Atkinson by the Act of Parliament'*. This was the third meeting requested in order to deal with any objections or claims to the dividing up and enclosing by interested parties of the Commons and Waste grounds in the said area. These enclosure meetings were frequently advertised all over the county and by 1816 tens of thousands of acres of land was enclosed in Cumberland.

As the road system increased Toll charges were set up to pay for the maintenance and repairs. These charges were paid at Toll Bars and Turnpike cottages that were built on most of the roads leading into the town or villages. These were generally situated about a mile or so outside. Although in some cases like Wigton there was a toll bar at East End, on the edge of the town and one at the south side at Southend as well as the toll cottages at Spittal and Waverton. The first toll cottages conformed to a rectangular style, but later more distinctive designs were built like some that still stand today. They were mainly single storey buildings, but one on this route to Whitehaven beside Workington Bridge at Calva Brow is a two storey building. These cottages were built with windows or a doorway that took full advantage of the approaching traffic in both directions. A toll bar, gate or chain was hung between posts across the road. A small gate was available for any pedestrians walking through. A lamp was required at night this would be attached to a bracket outside the cottage. The accommodation provided was simple, along with a garden plot and well for water. Besides male toll keepers many women operated these Turnpikes while their respective husbands worked as farmers or labourers nearby. In the early days they were not popular, drovers, travellers and the locals objected to paying the tolls requested for passing through with live stock or loaded wagons on their way to market. Some found other ways of getting into town unnoticed, but these would eventually be caught and face a stiff penalty.

Outside the toll cottages various charges were displayed. In 1824 an Act was passed that tolls from Carlisle via Wigton through to Cockermouth were to be charged as follows:

*For every horse, mule, ass or other beast drawing any coach, landau, berlin, Phaeton, curricle, chariot, chaise, calash, hearse, caravan, gig, chair, car or such like carriage, the sum of Four-pence.*

*For every horse or other beast drawing any waggon, wain, cart or other such like carriage, the fellies of the wheels whereof are of the breadth of four inches and a half and upwards, the sum of One-penny halfpenny.*

*For every horse or other beast drawing any waggon, wain, cart or other such like carriage, the fellies of the wheels whereof are of less breadth than four inches and a half, the sum of Two-pence.* (These narrow wheels did more damage to the road surface hence the higher toll).

*For every horse, mule or ass laden or unladen, and not drawing, the sum of One Penny; but that for every horse, mule or ass, or other beast drawing any cart or other carriage laden with lime to be used for manure only, and passing through any of the tollgates erected or to be erected by virtue hereof, there shall be demanded and paid the sum of One Penny and no more.*

*For every drove of oxen cows or neat cattle, the sum of Ten-pence per score, and so in proportion for any less number: And for every drove of hogs or pigs, calves, sheep or lambs, the sum of Five-pence per score, and so in proportion for any less number.*

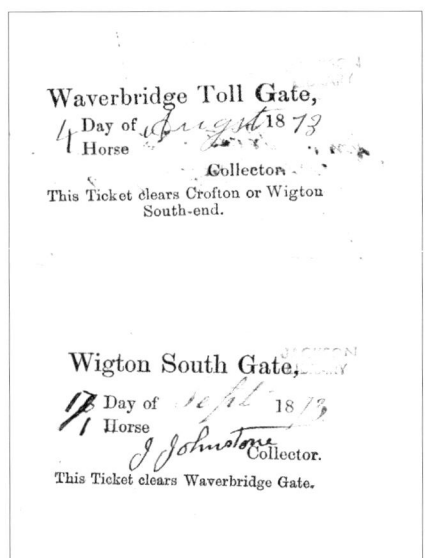

*Toll Gate Tickets - Wigton*
*by kind permission of Carlisle Library*

These tolls were to be demanded and taken before any animal or wagon was permitted to pass through the turnpike, tollgate or bar. A note or ticket indicating the payment and specifying the name of the Gate or Toll bar was given to all who wished to pass through by the Toll keeper. This ticket lasted from twelve o'clock at night till twelve o'clock the following night. Where a toll cottage was located at the edge of a town and a further toll bar existed in the town only one ticket was issued if the person was travelling through both tolls.

Stagecoach proprietors paid their tolls on a monthly basis, enabling the coaches to pass through the turnpikes without stopping. As the coach approached, the guard sounded his horn and the Toll keeper opened the gates and let them through.

The route from Carlisle through to Whitehaven went via Raffles, Moorhouses, Micklethwaite, Wigton, Waverton, West Newton and Allonby. The road then followed the coast from Maryport to Workington. Leaving Workington the route continued inland by way of Winscale Moor and Distington a wild crossing of open waste moor land and finally to Whitehaven. With much trading coming from these ports there was stiff competition for moving goods and passengers around the country quickly. Other routes opened up from Whitehaven, to Penrith and the south of Cumberland to link up with the main routes to Manchester, Birmingham and London. The 'Royal Sailor' stagecoach ran this route from Carlisle to Whitehaven from 1811 to 1842, where as some stagecoaches using other routes to Penrith, Cockermouth or Keswick only survived for short periods of time before they where changed or upgraded and renamed.

The running of a stagecoach was not a profitable business the various proprietors did not become millionaires, but they did see the need to convey the public around the country. With trade improving, merchants and businessmen required transport. The Post Office also required a reliable service to deliver their mail. Many people came as visitors to the area by stagecoach this enabled them to discover the delights of the Lake District and the surrounding Solway coast.

# Carlisle to Wigton - 12 miles
## Coaching and Wayside Inns in italics

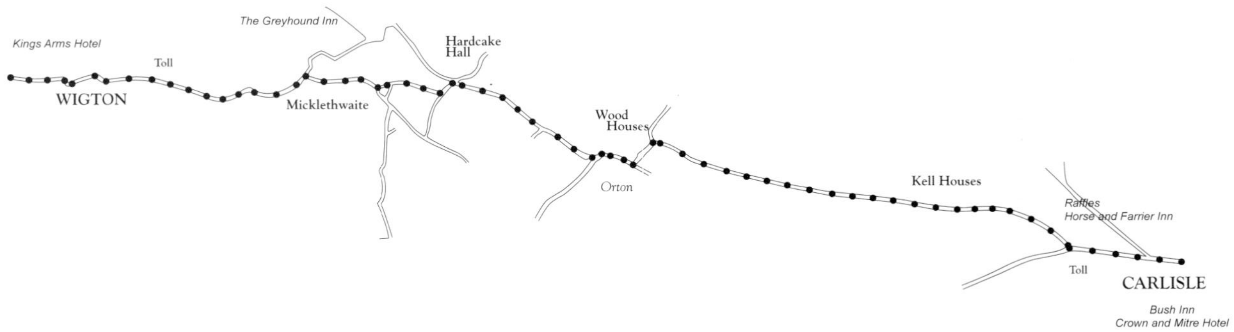

*Kings Arms Hotel*

Toll

WIGTON

Micklethwaite

*The Greyhound Inn*

Hardcake Hall

Wood Houses

Orton

Kell Houses

*Raffles*
*Horse and Farrier Inn*

Toll

CARLISLE

*Bush Inn*
*Crown and Mitre Hotel*

*The route taken by the 'Royal Sailor' stagecoach, from Carlisle to Wigton in 1811 (adapted from 1774 map)*

18

*Carlisle in 1846, by kind permission of Carlisle Library*

## Chapter Two

## 'THE ROYAL SAILOR' ROUTE

The name given to this stagecoach was probably derived by the historical topic of the day. William, Duke of Clarence the third son of George III joined the navy as a young man and served under Admiral Sir George Rodney during the American Revolution. Working his way through the ranks he achieved the status of Admiral in 1811. This would be much in the news and the proprietors of the new stage coach service would honour the Duke by naming the stagecoach after him. The fact that the coach would be calling at three Cumbrian ports along its route, Maryport, Workington and Whitehaven most probably also enhanced the idea of choosing the name the 'Royal Sailor'. In 1830 when William became William IV he was known as the 'sailor king'. Another stagecoach was named after him in the 1830's the 'Royal William' which ran between Newcastle and Berwick.

Royal Sailor Post Coach, from Carlisle to Whitehaven.

ON Monday the 8th of April, 1811, the ROYAL SAILOR commenced running every Day, (Sunday excepted) from the Bush Inn and Coffee House, Carlisle, alternately, at Nine o'Clock in the Morning, through Wigton, Allonby, Maryport, and Workington, &c. and arrives at Whitehaven about Five o'Clock the same Evening.

Leaves Whitehaven every Morning at Seven o'Clock, and arrives in Carlisle before the Departure of the Scotch Mails.                    (15)

*by kind permission of Carlisle Library*

The earliest record of the 'Royal Sailor' post coach service was advertised in the Carlisle Journal on March 22nd 1811. It was to commence running every day (Sundays excepted) from Monday 8th April from the Bush Inn and Coffee House, Carlisle, alternately, at nine o'clock in the morning. Stopping at Wigton, Allonby, Maryport and Workington, arriving at Whitehaven about five o'clock the same evening. A coach also left Whitehaven every morning at seven o'clock arriving in Carlisle before the departure of the Scotch Mail and other connecting coaches leaving for various destinations.

The 1811 Jollies Cumberland Directory gives a different time-table. This states that the '*Post Coach to Whitehaven, called the Royal Sailor leaves every Monday, Wednesday, and Friday morning at 8.o'clock; and arrives every Tuesday, Thursday, and Saturday afternoon, at 3 o'clock*. From Whitehaven the '*Royal Sailor to Carlisle, leaves from the Globe Inn, King Street, every day, at five o'clock in the morning, returns at five in the evening*. This all sounds very confusing so one can only assume that eventually the time-tables were readjusted once the coach service was up and running.

The following timetable in 1829 from Whitehaven to Carlisle gives an idea of the time it took between stages, including the changing of the horses and possible refreshment stops for the passengers.

| Carlisle | The Bush & Coffee House Inns | 8.30.am |
| Wigton | The Kings Arms & The Queens Head Inns – alternately | 10.30 am |

| Allonby | | 12.00 Noon |
|---|---|---|
| Maryport | The Golden Lion, Senhouse St. | 1.00 pm |
| Workington | The Green Dragon Inn | 2.30 pm |
| Whitehaven | The Black Lion Inn | 4.00 pm |

…………………..

| Whitehaven | The Black Lion Inn, King Street | 7.45 am |
|---|---|---|
| Workington | The Green Dragon Inn | 9.00 am |
| Maryport | The Golden Lion, Senhouse St. | 10.00 am |
| Allonby | | 11.00 am |
| Wigton | The Kings Arms & The Queens Head Inn – alternately | 1.30 pm |
| Carlisle | The Bush & Coffee House Inns - alternately | 4.00 pm |

The journey from Carlisle to Whitehaven took 7.1/2 hours, and the return journey took 8.¼ hours. With lighter faster coaches and better roads the journey times improved. But why the return journey took longer one can only wonder. Perhaps there were more hills to climb on the return journey.

The mail was always ready for the coaches that came in and after a short respite and a change of horses they continued their journeys to other parts of the country.

An early post office was situated in Blackfriars Lane at the rear of the Bush Inn, this later transferred to Blackfriars Street when the post master moved house. As the coach arrived a post boy quickly took the mail to the office accompanied by the mail guard where it was sorted and made ready for dispatch. One can imagine if the coach was running late what stress was put on the horses as they galloped the last few miles into Carlisle to catch the various out going coaches, not to mention the discomfort of the passengers as they were tossed about in the coach.

The arrival and departure of the stagecoaches outside the Bush Inn and the Crown and Mitre Hotel and Coffee House caused quite a scene in those early days. The stagecoaches would look magnificent all smartly turned out in their various coloured liveries with four or even six horses pulling them, their harnesses and brasses all gleaming. The coachman dressed in his great coat and high beaver hat, whip in hand with the guard beside him suitably dressed often armed with a pistol or blunderbus to protect the mail and passengers. There would be much hustle and bustle outside the hotels with passengers alighting from their journeys or departing. The hotel proprietors welcoming their guests, luggage being attended to and maids and servants from the hotels assisting. The ostlers and stable hands busy with changing the horses. People would also gather round to watch this spectacle of the stagecoaches arriving at a brisk pace from London, Manchester, Leeds, Newcastle or the north, and then to watch them leave to continue their journeys.

A very colourful scene with the all the ladies and gentlemen dressed in the fashions of the day, often influenced by the latest Paris designs. The ladies fashion at this time was of a simple classical style, draped bodices and skirts, for coach travel more suitable than large crinoline dresses. The hats were smaller more of a bonnet shape festooned with ribbons and flowers, showing the curls and ringlets. In cold weather long or three-quarter coats were worn trimmed with fur, and large fur muffs to keep the hands warm. The gentlemen were equally smartly dressed in tall top hats, waisted jackets and waistcoats, pantallons or breeches and knee length boots, the whole ensemble tightly fitting. For cold weather a heavy great coat was worn often with several shoulder capes.

The Bush Inn originally situated in Scotch Street in the 1700's moved to English Street in 1783. The square building was constructed around a paved courtyard with pump and water butts. At a later date the courtyard was roofed over and a building was added to the archway. The archway called the Bush Arch was situated over the

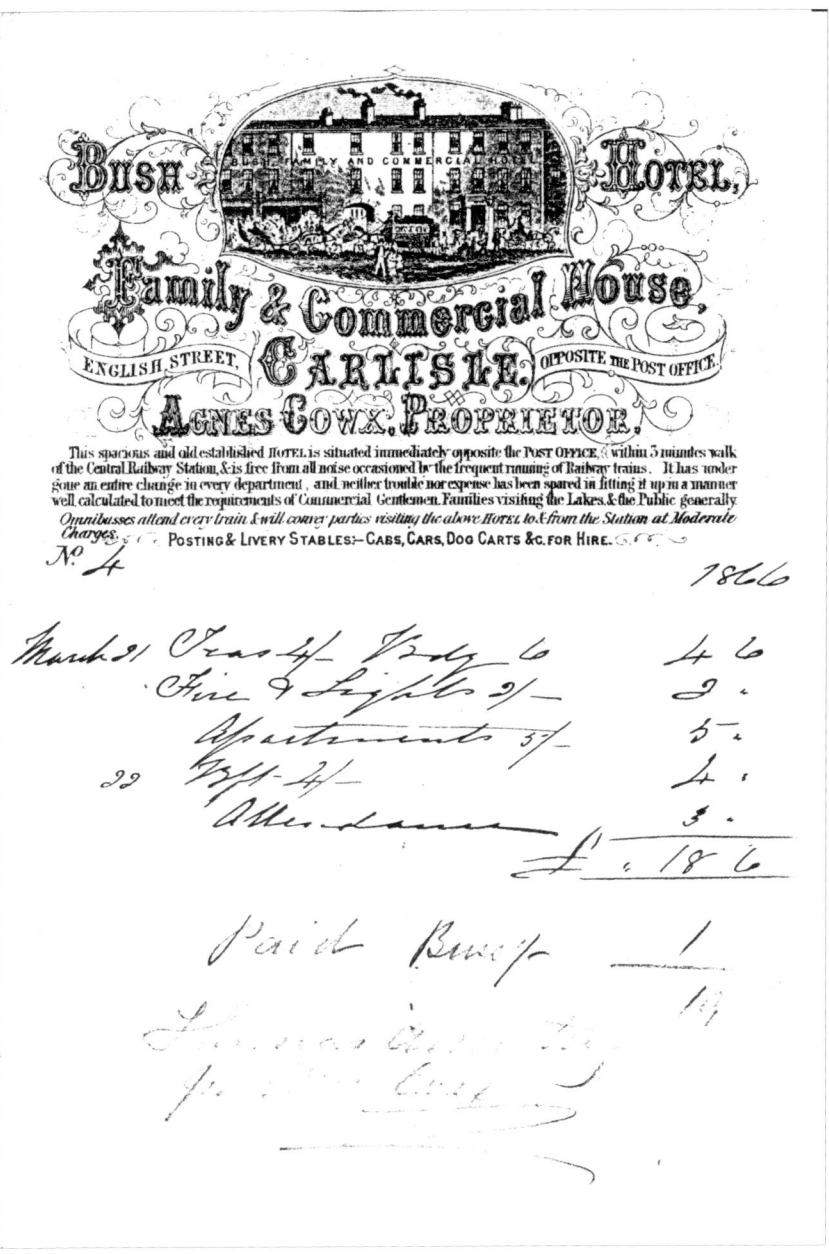

*The Bush Hotel, Carlisle by kind permission of Ashley Kendal*

now Viaduct Road. Mr T.Wilson in 1811 was the innkeeper and kept a good house. The Bush Inn was well known to be one of the best Hotels and Posting houses in the north of England. Many social and club activities were held, including balls and assemblies. The Justices of the Peace from the Quarter Sessions often continued their business while sampling the Bush Inns hospitality. Other functions were held to mark special occasions such as the opening of the canal from Carlisle to Port Carlisle in 1823 and the Newcastle to Carlisle railway line in 1838.

The Crown and Mitre Hotel and Coffee House proprietor was a Mr William Graham and this establishment was an equally good social gathering place and probably as old as the Bush Inn. Both establishments were built when the first stagecoaches started to appear on the scene. It is said that eleven mail coaches stopped at these two inns alternately, on Mondays, Wednesdays and Fridays, this was to help ease the traffic flow. One wonders how old Carlisle coped with all the traffic, the private coaches, post chaises and gigs etc. not to mention wagons delivering goods to various parts of the town. Animals being herded in to market, stalls about the town selling goods that had been brought in from the outlying farms and people milling around and going about their business.

The Bush Inn and the Crown and Mitre Hotel and Coffee House had a booking office each, run by the coach contractors where bookings were made and timetables kept for all the many coaches that travelled through Carlisle. There was stabling for eighty horses in the city, which supplied the various stage and mail coaches. These horses would be constantly on the move after they were sufficiently rested and fed. The

*by kind permission of Carlisle Library*

24

working life of a coach horse was roughly four years, and then they were sold on for other uses such as saddle horses or for farm work. In 1826 an advertisement in the Carlisle Journal states that fourteen horses, the property of Fairbairn and Wilson, were withdrawn from the Mail and other Coaches. *"All good goers, of superior action, quiet workers, true and steady drawers and each from 15 to 16 hands".* These horses would have served the best of their years pulling coaches around the country, a job that demanded all their strength. Being sold on for about £5, they could look forward to a quieter life, but it is doubtful if they ever got it.

HORSES FOR SALE.

TO BE SOLD BY AUCTION, opposite the Bush Inn, English-Street, CARLISLE, on SATURDAY, the 5th day of AUGUST, 1826, at one o'clock in the Afternoon, (by Mr. TELFORD,)

FOURTEEN HORSES, the Property of Messrs. FAIRBAIRN and WILSON, lately withdrawn from the Mail and other Coaches, in high condition, mostly young, all good goers, of superior action, quiet workers, true and steady drawers, and each from 15 to 16 hands high ; selling for no faults, but owing to the Proprietors having no further use for them. They are adapted for Saddle, Harness, or Farming purposes.

Such useful Horses of the above description are seldom offered for Sale in Carlisle.

Carlisle, July 28th, 1826.

*by kind permission of Carlisle Library*

There were several stagecoach builders in Carlisle, but it is not known who built the coaches for the Royal Sailor route. It could have been William Baty of Blackfriars Street, James Fairbairn of English Street or Thomas Wilson of Castle Street. James Fairbairn took over William Baty's premises in March 1811 after the later died aged 42 years. In 1827 James Fairburn's business was then taken over by Thomas Tweeddal who extended the company further as an advertisement dated 1st March 1827 records.

*COACH & HARNESS MAKERS. Thomas Tweeddal & Co. Most respectfully beg leave to intimate to the inhabitants of Carlisle, and the Public in general that they have taken and entered upon the Coach making business, and the premises of (and lately carried on by) Mr Fairbairn. Thomas Tweeddal & Co. purpose extending their business in all its branches, and hope by the strictest Punctuality, and the most moderate Charges, to secure the Patronage of those who may honour them with their Orders. From the Experience that Thomas Tweeddal has had in the very first Establishments in*

*London, they can assure the Public, that every Order entrusted to their care, shall be executed in the most approved and fashionable style. Who have on hand, for sale, a best light Phaeton with Barscuba seat in front to take off occasionally, and may be used with one or two horses; also a low double bodied Phaeton to go with one horse. A neat Stanhope Gig and Harness, little worse for wear, the property of a Gentleman, having no further use for it; three new Stanhope Gigs; a neat pony Gig; several second hand Gigs; three post Chaises; a neat two horse Coach, and an outside Jaunting Car, with or without Horses.*
*English Street, Carlisle. March 1, 1827.*

In 1831 Thomas Tweeddal went into partnership with a Thomas Barton and they continued with their business in Albert Square, off Blackfriars Street. In 1838 they built their first omnibus for the Bush Hotel.

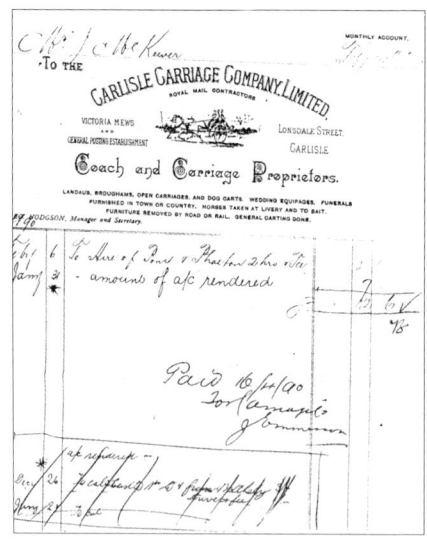

*by kind permission of Ashley Kendal*

Other stagecoach builders came along later advertising their skills, having worked in the finest of establishments in London and Edinburgh. With the increase of coaching there were many harness, saddle makers and coach smith's in Carlisle who were not short of trade.

Leaving the Bush Inn or the Crown and Mitre Hotel and Coffee House in the morning, the 'Royal Sailor' with passengers and post would make its way along English Street and Castle Street towards the Irish Gate, known also as the Caldew Gate to the open countryside in the direction of Wigton. Tolls were paid

*Irish Gate, Carlisle, by kind permission of Carlisle Library*

in and out at the city gates for goods, horses, cattle and sheep to be sold at the market. Also any packages conveyed by stagecoaches on their various routes. Here at the 'Gate' it would be a hive of activity with much coming and going, consequently many shops and inns were situated huddled together in this area around the inside and outside of the entrance. Traders plying their wares in 1811 were a butcher, grocer, tanner, two hat makers, nailor, miller, armourer, a stocking weaver and four inn keepers. One of the oldest inns The Black Bull stood here, rebuilt in the 1870's. Next door the Saracens Head was also rebuilt at this time. Both inns were eventually knocked together and renamed the Irish Gate Tavern in 1917. In 1972 it was demolished to make way for the Castle Way inner ring road. Overlooking the Irish Gate the Tile Tower of Carlisle Castle guarded the entrance. This tower still stands today.

Roads leading out of town were fairly good with hard surfaces as these were kept in a reasonable condition with revenue from the tolls collected. Crossing the River Caldew and passing the old brewery in Caldewgate, an iron foundry, a few houses and gardens the stagecoach stepped out towards the first tollgate.

This tollgate was situated where the Horse and Farrier Inn stands at the junction of two roads, the Wigton Road, and Orton Road at Raffles. The inn was first mentioned in 1697 and was situated across the road where a parade of shops now stands. It was reputed that in the 1800's 'cock fights' were held at this inn and a coach and four would take sportsmen from Carlisle out to enjoy the contests. Beside the inn was a blacksmith and stables. Every village and town had a blacksmith or farrier, always a busy man with horses to shoe and repairs to carriages, wagons, carts and farm equipment. He was also known to treat horses for their various ailments. With the ring of his hammer on the anvil and the glowing fire of the forge his workshop was often a friendly meeting place for the locals. These old smithies and stables can still be spotted around the countryside today, some are now renovated into modern homes and retaining

*Raffles Toll Gate - circa 1880's, Reproduced from J. Templeton's Collection*

their trademark as the 'Forge Cottage or The Smithy' etc.

The Raffles toll cottage stood between the roads, operating the two gates. It stood till 1883 when it was sold for £100 by the Cockermouth and Carlisle Turnpike Road Trustees, to the New Brewery Company in Carlisle which owned much of the land called Raffles. The building was eventually demolished in the early 1930's after the new Horse and Farrier inn had been built behind it in 1928.

The Orton Road in earlier times was the road from Carlisle to Wigton and named as such on maps and plans. A Turnpike Act of 1753 records the repairing and widening of the road from Carlisle to the market and sea port of Workington; through townships and villages called Raffles, Kellhouses, Woodhouses, Micklethwaite and Wigton, etc. Roads had become very bad and ruinous especially in winter season. Travellers and carriages could not pass without great difficulty and danger. A second Act in 1824 states for more effectual amending, improving and keeping in repair and to be made turnpike, the roads from the city of Carlisle to the market town of Cockermouth by way of Wigton. This was due to increased and constant travelling. The Thursby road to Wigton during these times by way of Newby West was less travelled being more open country. A gentleman wrote an article in the Citizen a fortnightly periodical in February 1830 about his walk from Carlisle to Wigton to attend a county meeting:

*'As I passed Suttle House, and arrived at the crossroads, with King-rigg on my left, I thought of those times when Dick Waite and his associates used to thump people's heads in the dark for the sake of what they had in their pockets. And Lord' it came across me, that in what a pretty pickle poor I should be if attacked by half-a-dozen of them on my return! These unpleasant morning reflections upon my possible evening's entertainment induced me to hurry past Newby Cross – through the gloomy plantations and across the dreary common'* ...

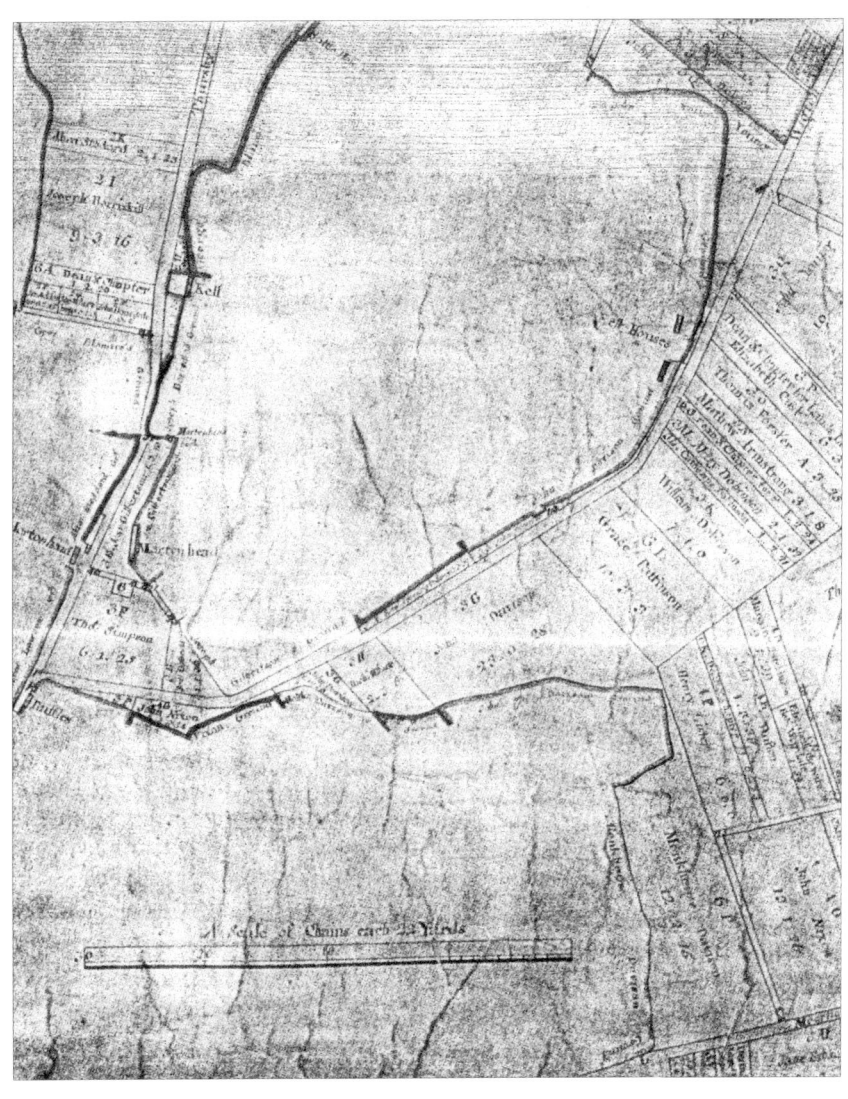

*Old map showing Raffles, Thursby Road & Wigton Road, early 1800's,*
*by kind permission of Carlisle Record Office*

The gentleman then continued towards Nealhouse and Thursby.

The earlier route used by travellers to Wigton from the Raffles toll gate, along Orton Road, passed the hamlet of Kell Houses (now Sandsfield Park estate) and continued on through Woodhouses, Hardcake Hall to Micklethwaite. These hamlets consisted of a few cottages and farms. This northerly route to Wigton had been requested by Sir Wastel Brisco of Crofton Hall. He owned a large estate with a deer park, woodlands, plantations and a well stocked lake with fish. His father Sir John Brisco had turned what was barren heath and morass to good agricultural land, which was highly cultivated and gave good quality crops. Consequently the Brisco family did not want the general public making their way through or transporting their goods and stock across the estate. So although there were roads on the estate the main road for general use i.e. wagons and coaches from Carlisle to Wigton had to make their way through the northerly part of the the Brisco lands, via Woodhouses, Hardcake Hall and through to Micklethwaite.

Along this part of the route the passengers sitting high on the stagecoach enjoyed good views towards the fells of the Lake District and in the other direction where the land was flat towards the Solway and across to the hills of Scotland.

In the Citizen periodical a passenger having booked a seat to Whitehaven on the Royal Sailor stagecoach related in an article in March 1822 that as the inside seats were taken he had to resort to the seat next to the coachman:

*'On the morning on which I left Carlisle, the rain poured from the heavens in pailfulls; and the inside of the Royal Sailor being filled with ladies, I had to content myself with a seat at the right elbow of "Fergy". The Sailor travels at a truly royal pace – slow and dignified as an alderman after a rent-day feast. One would almost think Fergy had sat for Geoffrey Crayon's picture of a*

*stage-coachman. He is familiar with all the boys and old women on the road; cheers his passengers with a song, and retails jests not peculiarly marked by any purity of language'.*

Later in August 1829 the Royal Sailor stagecoach met with an accident near Thursby as noted in the Citizen.

*'On Sunday the 9th the Royal Sailor coach was unfortunately overturned in descending a hill about a mile west of Thursby, by which the driver and several of the passengers were severely injured. The coachman had incautiously entrusted the reins to a young man of the name of Carrington, who was the direct cause of the accident. That part of the road, however, where it occurred is still extremely dangerous, and something ought to be done to prevent a recurrence of similar casualties'.*

The accident was also reported in the Cumberland Journal.

*'Coach Accident: On Sunday last, the coach which runs between Allonby and this city was over turned near Thursby. We understand that a young gentleman of the name of Brown was most seriously hurt, and narrowly escaped losing his life; and at present lies at Thursby in a dangerous state. A young woman called M. Glasson received some severe though not dangerous contusions. The coachman Archibold Hutton had one wrist dislocated and the other much hurt. There was a great number of passengers on the coach at that time, but none except those specified received any material injury. What ever the cause maybe, we always regret accidents of any kind happening, but we feel bound to state that the coachman was indirectly the cause of this, by permitting a young man by the name of Carrington to take the reins – a practice most deserving of reprobation, seeing what serious consequences ensue from it'.*

One would think that the coachman would have been severely reprimanded and possibly lost his job as a result of his foolhardiness in handing over the reins to a passenger.

The gentleman previously mentioned walking from Carlisle to Wigton further wrote in his article in the Citizen having heard about the stagecoach accident decided to stop and view the site.

*'Took a peep at the place where the Sailor coach was overthrown... horrid abyss!... wonder all were'nt knocked to atoms. It is really shameful that the danger of a repetition of such an accident should not be more carefully guarded against by the erection of a strong fence'.*

He also comments on the entrance to the village of Micklethwaite:

*'What a scandal is it to the Highway Trustees to have such a pass on their road at the gatestead at this village. Somebody will be killed there some of these days, and then it will be altered'.*

Having refreshed himself at the Greyhound Inn he continued on to Wigton.

The hamlet of Micklethwaite consisted of a farm, a few cottages, a smithy and an inn. Most hamlets and villages in North Cumberland had bars across the road at the entrances or exits to keep their cattle in at night and to deter unwanted persons. These bars consisted of upright oak posts with chains across the road. A watchman from each village looked after them. One was situated near the river Wampool and referred later as the Micklethwaite Gate. This main public route from the outskirts of Carlisle to Wigton was little more than a cart track with muddy conditions in the winter and dusty in the summer. It ran through this hamlet and across the river Wampool via a ford. Later a bridge was built here, still keeping the ford to one side for the cattle etc.

As traffic increased along this road in the early 1800's a farmer by the name of John Jefferson who owned premises and land in Micklethwaite

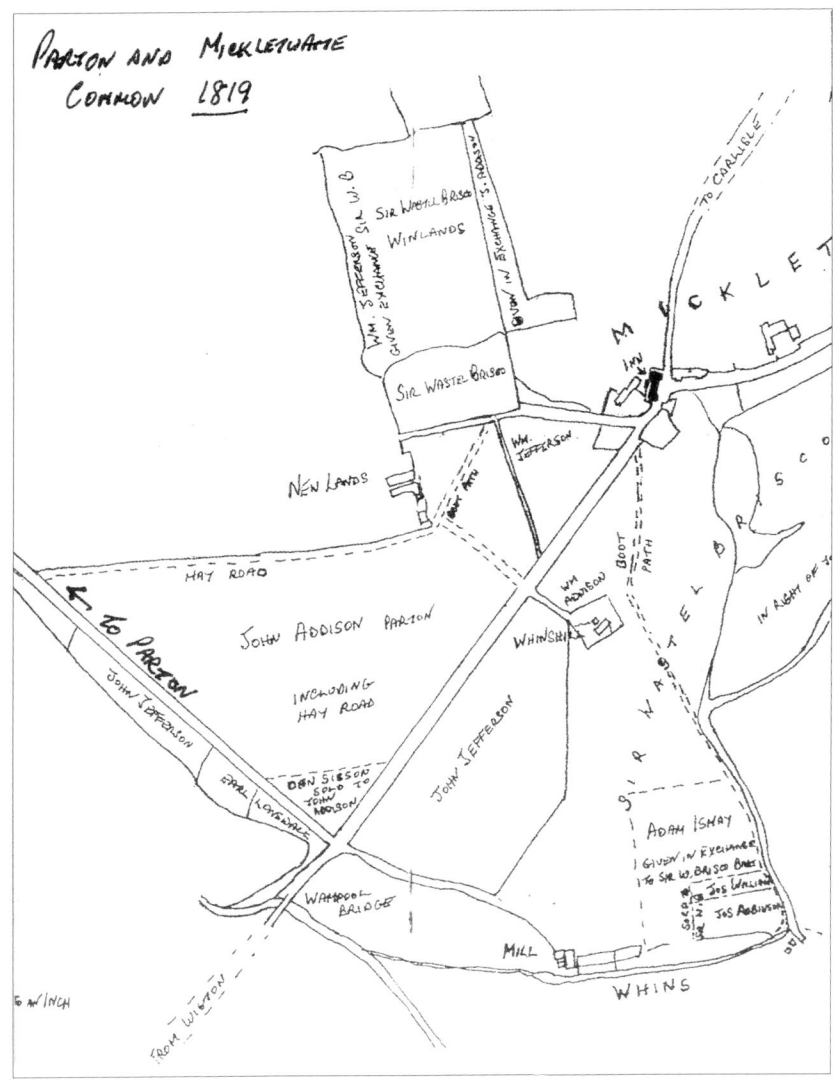

*Map of Parton & Micklethwaite Common 1819,*
*by kind permission of Carlisle Record Office*

obviously thought it prudent to open an ale house, this combined with his farming would improve his income and family's standard of living. In 1809 he is referred to as an innkeeper and later this inn is known as The Greyhound. The name was changed to The Brisco Arms in 1874 in honour of the late Sir Walter Brisco of Crofton Hall.

The 'Royal Sailor' stage coach may well have dropped off mail and the odd traveller here for the hamlets in the area. The Parton and Micklethwaite Common map of 1819 shows boot paths (some are known as rights of way today) and short cuts across the fields. The stagecoach on the Cockermouth route passed the main entrance to Crofton Hall on the other side of the estate and parcels and post may have been left at the gate house.

After leaving Micklethwaite the coach crossed the river Wampool via the bridge or the ford and on towards Wigton. According to the Turnpike Acts of 1753 there was to be erected a gate, turnpike or toll house, and later a side gate at Dockray. The hamlet of Dockray lay to the right of the road about a mile from the centre of Wigton. On the very early maps it shows that one could travel through Dockray to Kirkbride and Bowness. Now the road ends by the beck in Dockray. Perhaps the Turnpike Trust authorities thought that the public would slip through on this road to Wigton avoiding the Wampool Turnpike. Later it must have been decided to position the Turnpike at Spittal Cottage and dispense with the costs of running Wampool and Dockray Gates. Just before the Spittal Gate toll cottage on the opposite side of the road stood the Smithfield Inn. It has been a private house for the last sixty years. Spittal Cottage was last referred to as Spittal Gate in 1841 and was occupied by an agricultural labourer and his family, perhaps it was the wife who attended to the gate and toll duties. After 1851 it was named Spittal Cottage and tenanted by several other farm labourers and a blacksmith. It was finally demolished in the early 1980's and a new bungalow was built on the site.

As the stagecoach approached the town of Wigton, it passed through the East End Gates, which were situated at the turning into Kirklands. The terraced house at the end has an angled wall with windows situated for a good view of approaching traffic from Carlisle. Two turnstiles operated at these gates for pedestrians.

The coach was due to arrive at the Kings Arms Inn at half past ten in the morning. The mail would be exchanged and passengers would sample some mid morning refreshment as the horses were changed for the next stage of the journey. If the weather was bad and the coach was late this change of horses would only take a few minutes. Passengers would have to be content until they arrived at the next staging post.

*Kings Arms Hotel, Wigton, from the Trevor Grahamslaw Collection*

## Chapter Three

## WIGTON TO MARYPORT

With the increase of stagecoaches and other traffic the roads in Wigton were kept in good repair and many new bridges were built in the area. The common land around the town was becoming enclosed. Local farmers cultivated the land to a high standard. There was a great quantity of weaving being carried out in homes and small manufactures, producing many assorted cloths. With other trades and industries springing up Wigton became a busy town with a greatly increased population by the early 1800's.

Not only did the 'Royal Sailor' stop to change horses and collect passengers from the Kings Arm's Inn and the Queen's Head Inn alternately, but a coach or Post Chaise also stopped from Cockermouth en route to Carlisle on Tuesdays and returned on Wednesdays.

The Kings Arms a Commercial and Posting Inn, situated in Market Place along with the Queens Head Inn on the corner of King Street and New Street were both equally busy and popular. They had good stables with a change of horses for the stagecoaches and carriages and horses were also available for

THE GENTLEMEN of WIGTON and its Vicinity, Friends to the Independence of the County of Cumberland, intend Dining together at the KING'S ARMS INN, WIGTON, on FRIDAY, the 28th Day of APRIL, Instant.

Dinner on the Table at 3 o'Clock, and Tickets Six Shillings and Sixpence each, to be had at Mr. Irving's.

Gentlemen who intend Dining, are requested to leave their Names at the Bar, on or before the TUESDAY preceding.

T. BACKHOUSE, Esq. } STEWARDS.
J. HODGE, Esq.

N. B.—Owing to unavoidable Circumstances which would prevent the Attendance of a number of Gentlemen on the 27th, it has been thought proper to postpone the Day of Meeting till

*Friday, the 28th Instant.*

Wigton, April 19th, 1820.

*by kind permission of Carlisle Library*

hire.    Public meetings, entertainments and balls were held in the inns assembly rooms and a good hot meal was always available for travellers at either establishment.

The Kings Arms is known to have been in existence at least since 1767 when it is recorded that a county meeting of freeholders

# Wigton to Allonby - 12 miles
## Coaching and Wayside Inns in italics

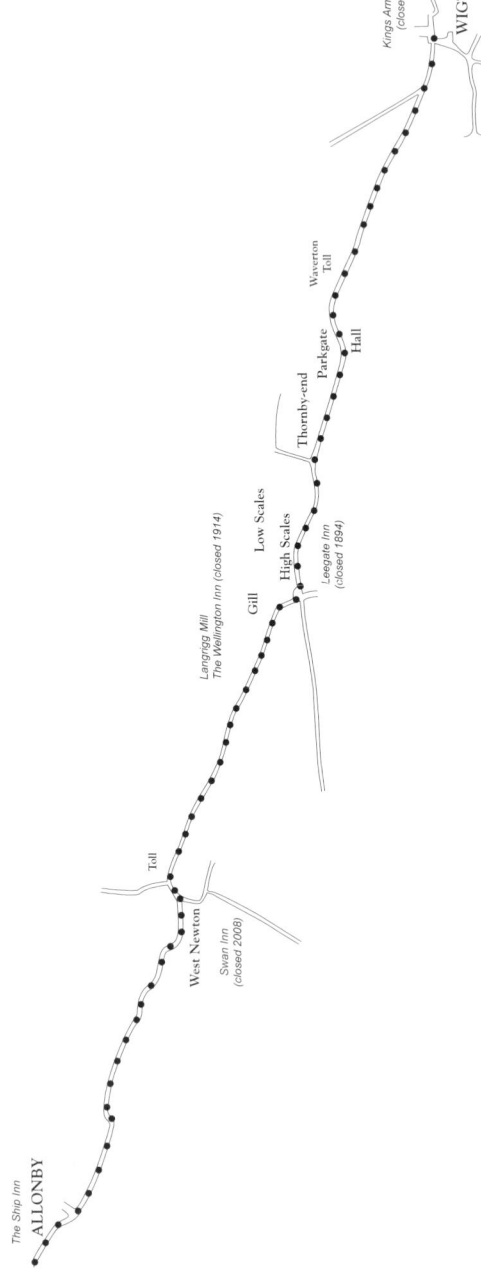

*The Ship Inn*
**ALLONBY**

Toll

West Newton
*Swan Inn
(closed 2008)*

*Langrigg Mill
The Wellington Inn (closed 1914)*

Gill

Low Scales

High Scales

*Leegate Inn
(closed 1894)*

Thornby-end

Parkgate

Waverton
Toll

Hall

*Kings Arms Inn
(closed)*

**WIGTON**

*The route taken by the 'Royal Sailor' stagecoach, from Wigton to Allonby in 1811 (adapted from 1774 map)*

nominated two candidates for the forthcoming general election. The earliest known landlord to be installed at the inn was Stephen Story in 1788. He was followed by a John Cumming in February 1804 and a further landlord in 1816. Now over 200 years of trading as a licensed Inn and Commercial Hotel the old inn stands forlornly boarded up awaiting a buyer and redevelopment.

In 1842 towards the end of the stage coach era these two Inns were damaged during the Chartists riots in Wigton. Both had their windows broken. Landlords Wm. Forrester and Jeremiah Smith were thought to have angered the mob by displaying unpopular posters. Widespread feeling was running high during this period as various activists had come to the town and spoken out at the meetings consequently inciting the local workers. Many of the local community had had their common rights taken away from them due to the 1832 Reform Act so were already resentful. Now they were expected to change their ways of working by new government laws to improve industry. During this time the 95th Regiment was billeted at the Queens Head to help quell the disturbances and worried shop and inn keepers kept their windows shuttered.

The Queens Heads earliest known proprietor in 1811 was Thomas Irving. It remained a coaching inn and hotel until late in the 1800's when a Mr George Bell changed the inn to a Temperance Hotel, a

*by kind permission of Carlisle Library*

Mrs Elizabeth Bell was recorded as the proprietress in 1897. The Royal Oak Hotel in West Street also became unlicensed. A social movement was afoot to try and cut down the excessive drinking in the town. Total abstainers wore a blue ribbon and were known as the 'Blue Ribbon Army' who had pledged to keep their promise. The last proprietor of the Queens Head as a temperance hotel was Mr C.Tennant. In 1906 and 1910 it is also recorded that the

'Ancient Order of Foresters' used the Queens Assembly rooms for their meetings. The secretary was Mr Robert Fisher. This ancient order began in 1813 in Yorkshire as the Royal Foresters and became an affiliated friendly society for mutual financial support. The meetings were run by working men for working men. Today the building is now shops with living accommodation above.

The 'Royal Sailor' its destination Whitehaven, would leave Wigton at 10.30 am by the Allonby road, now known as West Street. With fresh horses, and passengers having enjoyed some refreshments at one of the inns the stagecoach made its way out of town to Waverton passing through the toll gates known as Waverton Gate. The toll cottage still stands at the crossroads at the entrance to the village, now a white washed building and called 'The Toll Bar Cottage'.

Waverton was a small hamlet in those early days mainly consisting of a few cottages and farms. The White Horse was the village inn, now a private house. Parkgate at the south end of Waverton was suggested as a suitable site for a tollgate by the early turnpike trusts, but it must have been decided that the Wigton side of the village

*The Toll Gate at Waverton, from the Trevor Grahamslaw Collection*

was more suitable for a toll house. Parkgate was most probably the barred gate into the hamlet and like Micklethwaite kept closed at night to keep the cattle in and strangers out. No doubt a watchman was posted nearby.

The coach having passed through Parkgate proceeded south towards a small hamlet called Leegate. Here the Leegate Inn and farm stood. The Inn part of the farmhouse had a good cellar where the beer was kept cool in two cellar rooms. Two flights of steps going down to these cellars are well worn in the centre of each step. The beer would be brought up in jugs and handed through the stone hatch this is still in place in the kitchen today. This Inn was noted to be a halfway house for smugglers,

*Rear of Leegate House, circa 1830*
*by kind permission of Mr D. Atkinson*

bringing in whisky from over the border, they then moved on during the night. A coachman's house is situated at the rear of the courtyard. This may have been quite a thriving Inn in its day to warrant a resident coachman. Later when the railways and Leegate Station were being built, railwaymen and navies who cut the line that runs to the eastside of Leegate from Wigton to Maryport were known to frequent this Inn. Much ale was no doubt supped, hence the worn cellar steps. The occasional traveller may have alighted here along with local mail.

Continuing along past High Scales the old coaching route turned right at Sandraw and headed for Westnewton passing another local Inn called The Wellington. In 1829 William Parkin was the licensee.

*The Wellington Inn - Langrigg, circa 1903. Mrs Mary Jane Little sitting in the trap, Julie Little about 6yrs, by kind permission of Mr Wilson, Wellington House.*

The Inn probably takes its name from the Duke of Wellington who was known for ending the Napoleonic Wars and most notably defeating Napoleon at Waterloo in June 1815. He becoming prime minister in 1828. This inn continued with

*The Wellington Inn - Langrigg, 1790, by kind permission of Mr Wilson, Wellington House, Langrigg*

various licensees until sometime before 1906 when Mrs Mary Jane Little took over as the last inn keeper. She ran the inn until after 1914 when the inn was closed, possibly by the Control Board. The cellar today still has the stone racks for the beer barrels. It was also known that a whisky cask was fixed to the wall above with a measure jug, but this has long gone. The first floor of this inn was an open space where many dances and social occasions where held in Mrs Little's time. She catered and lodged farm workers and labourers that came to the area to work and drain the fields etc. and she also ran a pony and trap taxi service to Brayton Hall. The old inn has now been converted into two houses and still remains in the family.

Further along past the cross roads the coach passengers would see the sails of Langrigg corn mill turning in the wind. This mill dates back as far as 1810 similar to one in Wigton. In 1851 Jonathan Robinson was the miller here with his wife and two daughters. The cottage adjoining the miller's house is dated 1821 the millers house is much older and stood on its own originally. It has been recorded that the sails were removed before 1860 when the mill was worked alternatively by water and steam. At some stage in the

*'Langrigg Mill', picture taken before the present owner commenced restoration work in 1980*

1900's the internal mechanism was stripped out, the top capped and tiled and a chimney added to make the building habitable. After lying empty and ruinous for many years it was restored into a comfortable dwelling house in the early 1980's.

Along this route to Allonby the countryside was wild and open where passengers on the stagecoach could look out over moorland and mire to the north and south across to Brayton Hall the home of Lady Lawson whose husband Sir Wilfred Lawson met an untimely death in 1806.

A toll cottage known as the Westnewton Gate used to stand at the fork where the road meets the Silloth to Aspatria route before leading into Westnewton. This cottage was probably demolished to widen the road making the corner safer to view for oncoming modern traffic. All that is left to show that a building stood here is a well in the field   At this point the stagecoach would be out of sight, but the villagers would hear the sound of the coachman's horn before passing through the gate and on down into the village. It would be the highlight of the day to see this fine stagecoach in its painted livery colours and the four horses stopping or passing through on its way to Allonby. One can picture the children running to meet the stage and the villagers standing in doorways to watch it go by.

Westnewton was referred to as a neat village between two rivulets. It had three inns, The White Swan, The Queen's Head and The Marquis of Granby. The White Swan was situated in the centre on the left going towards Allonby. The Queen's Head was sited on the east side of the Aspatria road. This inn was closed by the Control Board in 1918. The Marquis of Granby Inn situated further along past the Swan Inn did not survive very long as it was only noted in the 1829 and 1847 directories. Although it was not a scheduled stopping place, no doubt passengers were picked up and dropped off occasionally when there was room on the coach. Leaving the

*The former Bush Hotel, Carlisle, rebuilt circa 1878,*
*now a branch of the National Westminster Bank.*

*The Crown & Mitre Hotel, Carlisle, where the old Coffee House*
*and Crown & Mitre Inn stood, rebuilt in the Edwardian style.*

*The Millennium Bridge over the Castleway, Carlisle,*
*now occupies the site of the old Irish Gate.*

*The present day junction of Wigton and Orton Roads,*
*where formerly the Raffles Toll Bar and Cottage stood.*

*The route along past Hardcake Hall.*

*The site of the Spittal Gate Toll Cottage now rebuilt.*

49

*This road at Dockray continued through to Kirkbride*
*in the 1700's, now ends at this bridge.*

*The East End Toll Gates where situated here in Wigton, the first cottage*
*where the Toll keeper lived had a good view towards Carlisle.*

*The Kings Arms Hotel in Wigton.*

*The Toll Bar Cottage, Waverton.*

*The Former White Horse Inn, Waverton, now a private Residence.*

*Leegate House, originally the inn.*

*Mile stones situated between Sandraw and Allonby.*

*Site of the Westnewton Toll Cottage, the well still in situ'.*

*This shows the new road and the old road to Aspatria at Westnewton.*
*The white house was the old Queen's Head Inn.*

*The Swan inn, Westnewton.*

*The road into Allonby from Westnewton.*

*Allonby, looking towards the Ship Inn.*

*The Saltpans at Crosscanonby.*

*Bank End Farm, circa 1716, situated at the side of the Old Coach Road.*

*The Old Coach Road, looking towards Bank End Farm and onwards to Allonby.*

*Ellengrove Villa built on the site of the old Maryport Toll Cottage Gate and Side Bar.*

*The Golden Lion Inn, Maryport*

*The Old Road from Maryport to Workington.*
*The route taken by the early stagecoaches.*

*The site of the Old Paper Mill, wooden bridge and ford crossing at Maryport.*

*The Toll Bar House, Calva Road, Workington.*

*The Green Dragon Hotel, Portland Square, Workington.*

*The Toll Bar Houses, Distington.*
*Named as a reminder of the turnpike.*

*The Globe Inn, Distington.*

*Bransty Toll Cottage, circa 1854. Built to replace its predecessor when the road was widened. The picture shows the old route over Bransty Brow.*

*The Globe Inn, Whitehaven, as it looks today.*

*A typical stagecoach in York Castle Museum, built about 1820.*

*Langrigg Mill, as it may have looked in its early working life, circa 1815*

village and out into the countryside the coachman would crack his whip and make up for lost time knowing the horses would be changed again at the next stop. Three and a half miles along this rough track lay Allonby and the coast. In summer time a dusty route to travel and in the bleak winter the sea winds would cut across the flat plain chilling the bones. The coachman would be very glad of his great coat and beaver hat. In the grass verge between Sandraw crossroads and Allonby are two old milestones showing the mileage from Wigton to Workington. They are still kept freshly painted today. As the road approaches the first cottages at Allonby one can see how narrow some streets were. The road is still only a modern day car width.

In the early days Allonby consisted of a few fishermen's cottages. It is situated ten miles west of Wigton and five miles north of Maryport. Gradually it became known as a fashionable bathing place with sands and a grassy promenade. Other houses sprang up and the little seaside village had numerous visitors. Hence the need for the stagecoach to make it a stopping place. Here the travellers would alight from the coach filling their lungs with the sea air

Looking North.
The Wrench Series, No. 5114    Christmas 1903.

before going into The Ship Inn for their lunch. By 1829 there were other public houses, The Queen's Head, The Sun Inn, The London Apprentice, The New Inn and The Greyhound. But the Ship Inn was known as the coaching inn. The stables were situated at the side of the building, now the Public Bar, with a further building at the back where coaches and traps were kept for hiring out. There was not a road as such, but an open area along the front, just dirt and grit, dusty in the summer and wet and muddy in the winter. The mail was dropped here and collected either on route for Whitehaven or on the return journey to Carlisle.

A young lady aged twelve, Mary Ferguson, stayed in Allonby with her brothers and sisters in June 1820 she writes home in a letter sent by coach, *"We have been bathing it was very pleasant, a great number of people were bathing today"*. The weather appeared to be quite hot at times. The young family had been sent along with their nurse for a holiday from Carlisle.

With a change of horses and passengers refreshed the stagecoach made its way through the ford across the beck. Later in the 1800's a suitable bridge was built to take the traffic of the day, but at this time coaches used the ford. A certain gentleman wrote in to the local Maryport newspaper in 1842 expressing concern regarding the state of the narrow bridge beside the ford.

*'Sir,- Having during the last five years frequently had occasion to visit the neat little town of Allonby, where hundreds annually resort to reap the benefits of salt water and pure air, I was much surprised to see some parts of the delightful place rather in a neglected state; but my attention was more especially attracted to an old narrow bridge, in such a state of repair, that well might 'twa wheel-barrows tremble when they meet.' Its situation is awkward and its dimensions so limited that it scarcely has the appearance of a thoroughfare. A friend of mine once approaching it, suddenly pulled up, woefully afraid of running through a window at the opposite end, where sat*

*two well-dressed females. So forbidding is its appearance from every point of view, that almost every variety of conveyance from a Coach to a Donkey cart takes the ford on either side rather than risk and trouble of driving over it, for it holds at defiance 'wo-hop' and jee-o'. As a public thoroughfare it is nearly forsaken and is now a favourite station for idlers and loungers of every denomination who usually assemble upon the centre of it to talk of the weather, scate-fish and codlings to the great annoyance of all who may have to thread their way through the motley group. In short it is in a dangerous state, and whoever will look and judge for himself, will scarcely be foolhardy enough to risk his neck upon it. Should the authorities conclude to remove the old fabrick, with the nuisance adjoining I may, perhaps at some future period give an opinion respecting the site and construction of a new one.'*

Continuing along the track towards the toll gate cottage, this stood on the coast side of the road just before the church. Later in the century the cottage was demolished and a house now stands on its site. The route follows the coast towards Maryport. Passengers would enjoy fine views on a good day of the Scottish coastline, Criffel and Southerness. But on cold wet days they would be only to happy to roll down the leather curtains and try to stay warm and dry inside, whilst thinking of those passengers sitting huddled together on top with their collars turned up and heads down against the wind and rain.

Along this road the coach would pass the Crosscanonby Saltpans. The saltpans lay beside the road on the coast side and on the opposite side the cottages and a stable for the salters. These saltpans where worked from 1634 to late 1700's. By the middle of the 1800's the cottages had been made into an inn locally known as the Solway Inn. In the 1861 Directory a Beattie Alphonso was referred to as the beer retailer on the 'seaside' of Crosscanonby. It did not exist for very long. This stretch of coast line from Allonby to Maryport was rife with smugglers bringing in their contraband in the dead of night and spiriting it away to some lonely secret store at an inland farm or inn later to be sold on. A local customs man or 'Riding Officer' from Maryport patrolled this coast line. A very precarious job, as the smugglers were known as highly dangerous to apprehend.

According to papers written by Humphrey Senhouse in 1790 there were two routes into Maryport from Allonby. One route followed the coast line to Bank End Farm owned by the Senhouse family and shows a date of 1716 over the door. The route then turned inland towards the Netherhall estate and into the town of Maryport. The other route the shorter of the two continued along past Bank End Farm following the coast towards Maryport and the harbour. A short distance from the farmhouse, along this coast road are the remains of what was thought to be an old toll cottage. It could still be seen early last century. The route continued along the shore line under the escarpment of Pipeherd Hill and the remains of the old Roman fort 'Volantium' and on towards the edge of the town and the harbour of Maryport. The road leading into the town and harbour at this point was King Street, where in 1811 many businesses traded, including five inns, timber merchants, ship chandlers, nailors and coopers. The Golden Lion coaching inn still stands today overlooking the harbour at Shipping Brow, but has been empty and boarded up for some time, awaiting development.

There appeared to be some controversy of the inland route and the coastal road to Maryport. In his papers Humphrey Senhouse of Netherhall local land owner and industrialist whose father named the town of Maryport after his wife Mary appeared to be concerned about the coast road as the cost of any repairs will fall heavily on him and the distance gained in the shorter route he thought to be trifling.

*'Besides these two Highways, which are indisputably such, there is another road of a more doubtful nature, which leads from Bankend along the sea shore to Maryport. It is certain that for time immemorial people travelling from Allonby and other places*

*to the market town of Workington and elsewhere have only gone
from Bankend to Rysay along the sand between the high and low
water marks, but have also passed over the lands adjoining to the
beach.*

*This too is the nearest way from Bankend to Maryport, and in
some of the earliest Grants of parcels of ground for the purpose
of building near the Harbour which were signed by the late Mr
Senhouse, it is descriptively mentioned as the Highway and leading
from Ellenfoot otherwise Maryport to Allonby by the sea shore. But
on the other hand there is the strongest reason to believe that the
inland road from Bankend over the County Bridge is the true course
of the ancient Highway'.*

*But now since, in consequence thereof, much damage has been done
to the coast and the road itself is in some places intirely washed
away and in others is threatened with a similar destruction, this
very road indited as out of repair and the inhabitants of the northern
sides of Maryport though they live upon the same estate and in
the same quarter of this parish, though they enjoy every benefit
of the harbour and every advantage of the roads in common with
the Lord of the manor, are nevertheless endeavouring to throw the
whole burden of the repair of this and other ancient Highways in
the quarter intirely upon him alone, and with this view have entered
into a covenant, and signed an Article to stand by one another'.*

The coast road at some stage must have been repaired for traffic
continued to use it. Perhaps the stage coach only used this route
in good weather as a short cut to the town, but in bad conditions
preferred the inland route past the Netherhall estate. Later in 1823
when many new roads and bridges were being upgraded and built,
a new road was constructed from the Allonby coast road just past
the salt pans that ran inland more or less parallel to the old road and
joined the Aspatria road into Maryport near to the entrance of the
Netherhall estate.

*The Toll Cottage at Ellengrove, circa 1891, by kind permission of Keith Thompson*

At this junction an area later known as Ellengrove a Toll cottage was built to serve both the Aspatria road and the Allonby road into Maryport. As road surfaces improved the stagecoaches preferred the inland route. The Turnpike toll cottage stood until the 1890's. Known as the Maryport Gate and Side Bar. Like many others its function as a Turnpike ended later that century and it was demolished. The Ellengrove Villa was built in its place, which stands today.

As the stagecoach passed through this turnpike it followed the road past Netherhall and into the town of Maryport to the Golden Lion Inn.

# Allonby to Maryport - 5 miles
## and Maryport to Workington - 6 miles
### Coaching and Wayside Inns in italics

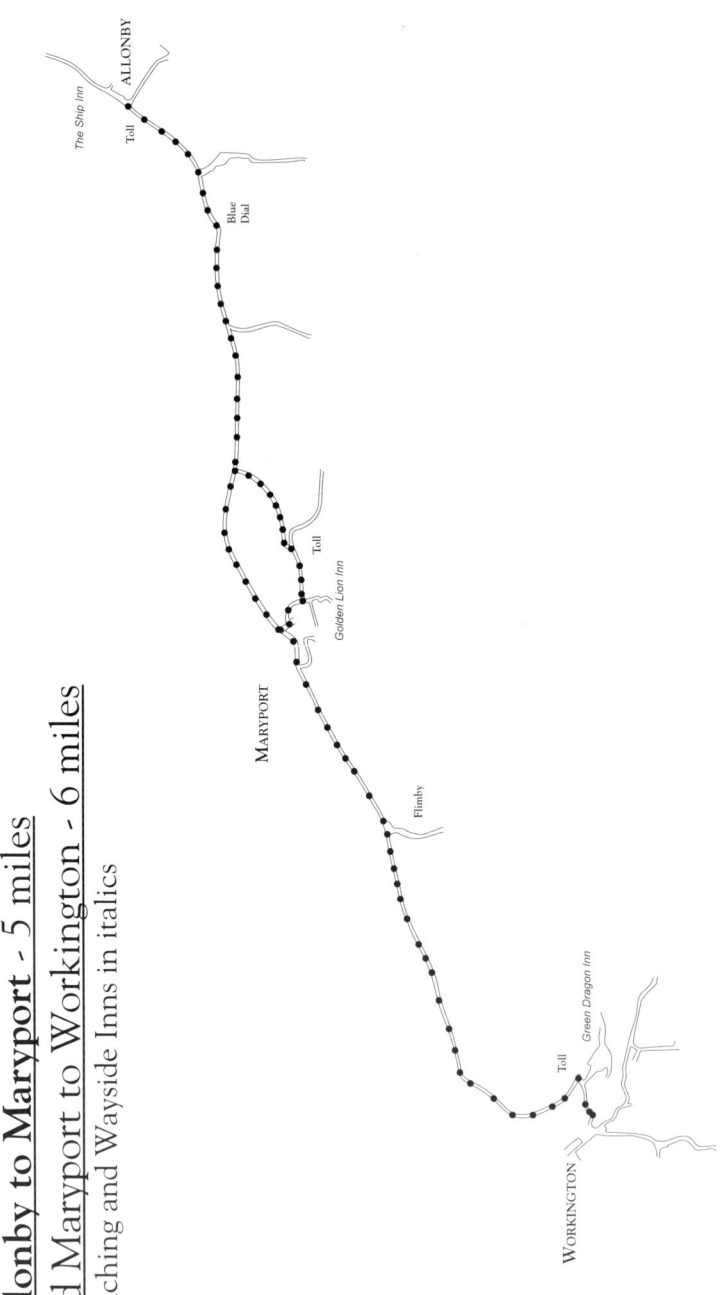

ALLONBY

The Ship Inn

Toll

Blue Dial

Toll

Golden Lion Inn

MARYPORT

Flimby

Toll

Green Dragon Inn

WORKINGTON

*The route taken by the 'Royal Sailor' stagecoach, from Allonby to Workington in 1811, with the new route (lower) after 1823 (adapted from 1774 map)*

*Shipping Brow, Maryport, circa 1900, by kind permission of Carlisle Library*

## Chapter Four

## THE NEXT STAGE TO WORKINGTON

In early 1700 Maryport or 'Ellenfoot' as it was first called was just a small hamlet of a few fishing huts, and a natural harbour that gave shelter to various small vessels. The first house to be built here overlooking the harbour was by the Senhouse family for a farmer. It was called 'Valentia House'. The farm had stables, outhouses and land. Above one of the stable windows the date 1719 and the initials of Humphrey Senhouse Lord of the Manor and his wife are inscribed. Also on one of the windows the words 'Licensed to let Post Horses'. The earliest reference to this farmhouse was in some deeds of 1752 when it was leased from Mr Senhouse to Mr Pape. It changed hands and was leased out several times over the next 30 years. By 1816 it became the principal inn in Maryport and known as the Golden Lion.

When the 'Royal Sailor' stagecoach first called at this inn on its way to Workington in 1811 the innkeeper was a Thomas Jackson. But in a will made by Hannah Wright it states she was in residence and wished to leave her estate to her brother. She appeared to have many strings to her bow. She was a Tallow Chandler and Grocer Tea Dealer. We suppose she also ran the inn for guests. The will states there was a candle house at the rear of the inn where candles were made for sale.

*Golden Lion Inn, Maryport, early 1900's, by kind permission of Philip Cueto*

By 1834, the land and property had been divided into several tenures and occupancies. A kitchen was added, a wash house, pantry and privy. Also running water! Business must have been very good in those times for all these 'then' modern facilities to be added. The town had grown considerably in the last fifty years and the Golden Lion Inn was used for social events and meetings. The stagecoach brought many visitors, merchants and business men to the town, not to mention a few famous names such as Fletcher Christian, William Wordsworth, George Stephenson, Charles Dickens and Wilkie Collins, where they may have stayed or partaken of the hospitality at this popular inn.

In 1829 Maryport was considered a neat and modern built market town and seaport with a healthy situation at the mouth of the river Ellen. In the last 80 years it had grown to some importance due mainly to the Senhouse family the Lords of the manor, over several generations. The town expanded with the coal trade on the Senhouse

*Maryport, 1815, by kind permission of Carlisle Library*

estate and eventually by this time over 650 houses had been built. The harbour had improved from originally being just wooden piers. By this time it held 134 ships many of these exported coal to Ireland and Scotland. Other vessels traded to America, West Indies and the Baltic. The local fishing fleet went out, weather permitting, for their catch of herring known to be plentiful in these waters. With all this shipping many trades had sprung up around the harbour making it a hive of activity.

The Royal Sailor arriving at the Golden Lion Inn may have changed horses here, but normally they were hitched up to carry out a journey of about twelve to fifteen miles. Having changed to fresh horses at the Ship Inn in Allonby they would have continued along the next seven miles from Maryport to Workington where another fresh set would be waiting. Here at the Golden Lion Inn those passengers who were continuing their journey would take some light refreshment while enjoying the view from the windows that looked out over the busy harbour. The stagecoach left at one o'clock along what was known as the old Workington road, this ran past the Queens Head Inn, along the river Ellen from the harbour, skirting the side of the Mote Hill and out towards what was called the 'tongue' where a Paper Mill was situated. Here a ford was used to cross the river between tides. According to Mr Senhouse in his writings he reported that coaches had great difficulty in crossing the ford due to the steepness of the banks and the river being tidal.

*'The County Bridge can be passed in every season and at every hour, but the ford by the Paper Mill cannot be crossed, when either the tide or the river is high. In either of these cases there is no passage even from one side of Maryport to the other without having recourse to the County Bridge'.*

Consequently the stagecoach at high tide continued its journey the longer way out of town via the County Bridge on the east side where a Toll Gate Cottage stood on the Ellenborough road before

74

turning towards Workington. A Side Gate was erected at Risehow, but with the coming of the railway this soon disappeared.

The seaward side on the out skirts of this part of Maryport were flat and sandy. This coastal route was wild and barren in winter with the sea hurtling itself onto the beaches and sand dunes and with nothing to stop the force of the wind battering the sides of the coach, the horses strained their heads into the wind, their manes and tails flying. Not many passengers would try their luck by travelling on top of the coach, despite the cheapness of these precarious seats. It was as much as the stagecoach driver could do to stay in his seat and control the horses in front of him. During the summer months this part of the journey afforded fine views to the north and south and across to the hills of Cumberland.

Population was sparse along this coastline with one or two farms and the remains of old Salt Pans. It was along this road that a highway robbery occurred in 1843.

*'On Saturday night last as Captain Nicholson of Maryport was proceeding at a late hour from Workington to that place, he was attacked by three men, who leapt upon him from behind a hedge, and demanded his money. They were armed with a bludgeon and Captain Nicholson being provided with a stout stick, and not at all inclined to yield on easy terms a fierce battle ensued. But just as the stout hearted chap was likely to be over powered, the sound of a horse and gig coming along the road was heard, Capt. Nicholson seized the opportunity to call out Murder! Robbery! The villains fled with out effecting their purpose'.*

The old village of Flimby could be seen on the hill towards Dearham Moor. One can imagine that occasionally a passenger would be dropped off here to walk the rest of the way up to the village, or be picked up to attend some business in Workington. As the stagecoach approached Workington the road followed the river

Derwent inland until it met the Seaton road at a stone bridge built about 1750. From this side of the river the bridge was the only way into the town. Here the Workington Turnpike Gate House stands controlling the two roads and the bridge. The house was built with many windows and a porch door at the front enabling the toll keeper to see in every direction. The road continued past Workington Hall, the seat of the Curwen family and along into the cobbled area of Portland Square to the Green Dragon Inn.

Workington in the early days of 1811 extended about a mile along the south side of the river Derwent, a rather straggly market town with narrow streets and cobbles and it was also a busy sea port. In 1810 it is stated that 134 ships belonged to the port. Many fine ships were built here providing work for the growing town. The principal export trade was coal to Ireland and lime to Scotland. A few vessels took their cargo to America and the Baltics. In exchange they brought back fine timber, hemp for rope making and cloth. The iron industry was also thriving with many furnaces and foundries to be found in the surrounding area.

All this busy trading brought merchants to Workington and the other towns and ports along the Solway coast. Not only did they come by way of the 'Royal Sailor' stagecoach from Carlisle, which arrived about half past two o'clock in the afternoon at the Green Dragon Inn in Portland Square. But on alternate days by other routes such as Kendal on the 'Good Intent', and 'The Volunteer' from Penrith, which travelled via Keswick and Cockermouth arriving at half past six in the evening. The busiest time would be in the morning when the 'Royal Sailor' coach came in from Whitehaven and left for the return journey to Carlisle at nine o'clock. The 'Good Intent' and the 'Volunteer' coaches then arrived also from Whitehaven and left an hour later at ten o'clock. The cobbled surface of the fashionable Portland Square would ring to the sound of the coach wheels and horses hooves as they rode to and from the Green Dragon Inn.

Workington from Calva Brow

By 1829 'The Good Intent' and 'The Volunteer' were replaced by 'The Royal Mail' and 'The Defiance' coaches respectively. Perhaps these two new coaches were faster as the arrival and departure times were readjusted. The design and building of coaches was improving all the time making them stronger and better sprung and lighter to handle with only four seats inside, and possibly eight seats outside on top, these where referred to as Fast Coaches. The coach proprietors must have been quite happy with the 'Royal Sailor' as it continued using the Carlisle to Whitehaven route until 1843. They no doubt also upgraded their coaches from time to time.

One can imagine how busy Portland Square was with the changing of passengers and baggage, some passengers just alighting for refreshment to give them sustenance for the last stage of the journey, and others leaving the coaches and being picked up by the waiting Chaises and Traps to continue to their final destinations, to their places of business or their homes. The stable boys ready to change the horses from the stables in Fox Lane or Stony Lane as it was once called and hitched up to the waiting coach. These stables not only housed horses for the stagecoaches, but for the local hearse and other carriages.

*Portland Square, Workington, circa 1900, by kind permission of Carlisle Library*

The Green Dragon and post house is one of the oldest in Workington and is thought to date back to 1728. In the 1800's it would have been much enlarged to match the growing town, with a large staff of maids, cooks and 'boots', stable and livery boys. The innkeeper Henry Salkeld in 1811 would welcome the visitors to Workington. The inn in those days was the centre for many of the town's activities. The local gentry, some of whom consisted of wealthy sea captains, attorneys and surgeons from the grand houses around the Square met to exchange the topics of the day. Merchants came to the inn to transact commercial business and many a handshake would take place to clinch a deal.

The Inn was also the meeting place for various property sales which were duly notified in the local newspapers. In 1820 it appears Hannah Salkeld was the proprietress at the inn as the following advertisement in the Whitehaven Gazette shows the sale of a Brewery and Dwelling House nearby:

*'TO BE PEREMPTORILY SOLD, in Public Sale at the house of Mrs Hannah Salkeld the Sign of the Green Dragon, in WORKINGTON, in the County of Cumberland, in the Evening of Monday the Fifteenth Day*

*of May next One Thousand Eight Hundred and Twenty, either together or separately (unless Previously disposed of by Private Contract, of which Notice will be given) precisely at Six o'Clock; - all that Large and Extensive BREWERY, commonly called the OLD BREWERY, with the commodious Buildings thereunto belonging, situated under the Brow, in Workington on aforesaid, consisting of a well built Dwelling House and Parcel of Ground behind, a Brew-house, Milk-house, Cellars, Offices, a Boiler capable of containing 700 Gallons, a good Malt-kiln of the dimensions of 19 feet, 2 inches by 17 feet, 2 inches; Granaries, Rooms for stowing Malt, Stable, Hayloft, Yard and every convenience for carrying on the Brewing and Malting business upon a very extensive scale:*

*Also Eight Good Substantial Built Dwelling Houses, and School-house, adjoining the Brewery, all Let to respectable Tenants.*

*This Brewery is most eligibly situated, is supplied with Water from an adjoining Stream, flowing from the River Derwent, and is an old established Concern, having been carried on for Seventy Years last past. Workington, April 24th 1820.*

This old brewery no doubt supplied the Green Dragon and many of the other old inns in Workington with their ale during these very early times.


After a brief respite at the inn the passengers boarded the coach, some of whom had travelled from Carlisle would be relieved to know the last part of the journey would soon be over as the coach was due to arrive in Whitehaven at five o'clock. The streets out of Portland Square are all narrow one can only assume that the coach would leave by Cavendish Street of Christian Street to make its way out of town.

# Workington to Whitehaven - 8 miles
## Coaching and Wayside Inns in italics

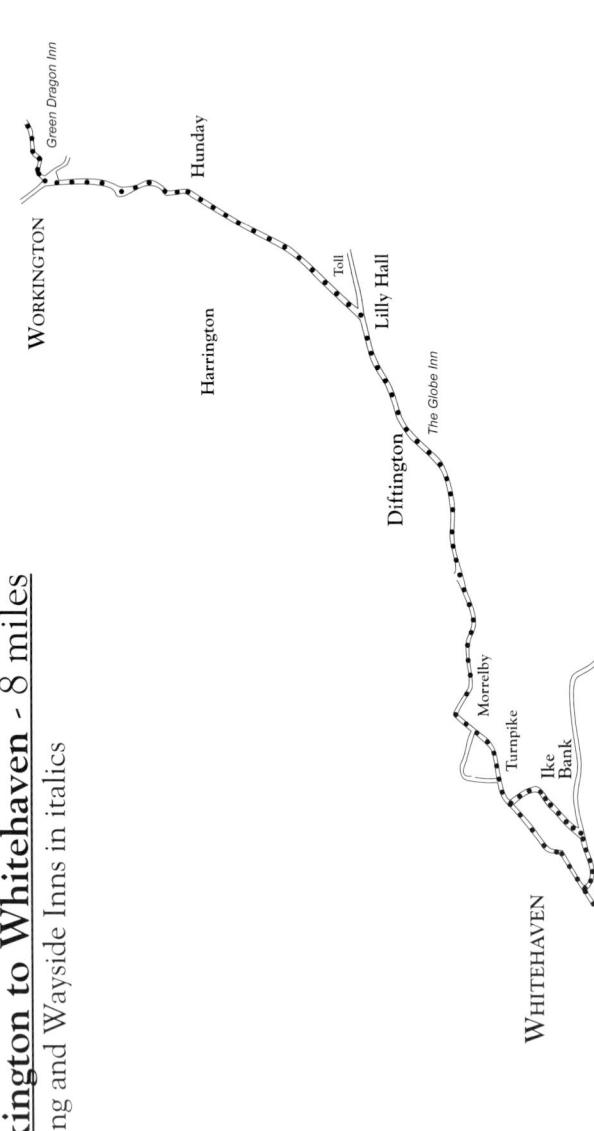

WORKINGTON

*Green Dragon Inn*

Hunday

Harrington

Toll

Lilly Hall

Diffrington

*The Globe Inn*

Morrelby

Turnpike

Ike Bank

*Globe Hotel*
*Black Lion Inn*

WHITEHAVEN

*The route taken by the 'Royal Sailor' stagecoach in 1811, a later new route also shown (adapted from 1774 map)*

# Chapter Five

## WORKINGTON TO BRANSTY

The stagecoach heading out of Workington made its way in a southerly direction passing the gates to Schoose Farm where John Christian Curwen of Workington Hall introduced new experimental methods of farming. Passengers in the coach would see much activity in the fields and the land around this farm, as John Curwen employed a large work force and at harvest times as many as 300 workers or more were needed to bring in the harvest. These extra harvest hands were paid three shillings a day plus meat and drink. It may have seemed a good wage at that time, but work was intermittent and they probably had to survive the winter before finding work again at the next hiring day fair.

The road continues over open country and across the wild moorland of Winscales to meet up at the junction of the Cockermouth to Whitehaven road at Lilly Hall. Further along, the road meets with

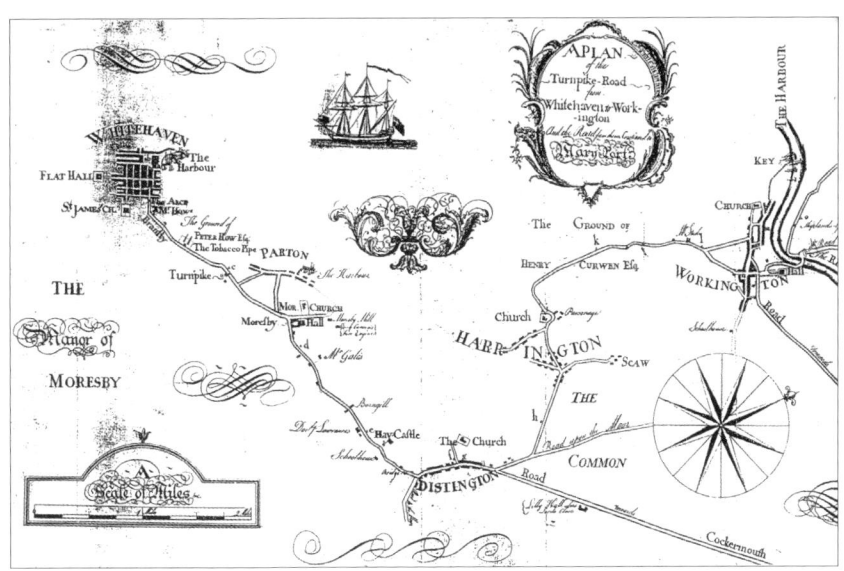

*Section of a turnpike road, circa 1760, showing the old route past the Tobacco Pipes, Bransty, by kind permission of Mr P. J. Scott-Plummer*

the High Harrington road where a turnpike was situated just north of the village of Distington. The toll cottage was still standing in the early 1950's, around this time the Cockermouth high road was widened to take today's modern traffic consequently the toll cottage was demolished. Later, a row of terraced houses was named the Toll Bar Houses as a reminder of former times. The old toll cottage operated both the Cockermouth road and the side road to the seaport of Harrington. In the late 1700's a Turnpike route was proposed from Workington along the coast to Harrington and round to meet the Cockermouth road. It is not known if the stagecoach ever took this route when the new road was in place, probably not, as they kept a tight timetable and this new road would have increased the journey time.

Generally the roads between Maryport, Workington and Whitehaven were kept in reasonable condition because of the considerable traffic that used them from the various local mines, quarries and lime kilns. Although many of the products that came from these sources went by sea, a good quantity went by wagon and packhorse to other parts of the county, together with goods being shipped in. The owners of most of these trading companies looked after the roads they used the most. By today's standards they were still not very good. Wagons and coaches could get bogged down on a wet day and would have to be dragged out by a string of horses and passengers had a rough bumpy journey. The roads gradually improved however with the help of Thomas Telford and John Loudon McAdam, the road and bridge engineers who came along about this time.

Like other villages in Cumberland in the late 1700's the village of Distington was known to have had at least one gate across its thoroughfare to keep the cattle in at night and any unwanted strangers out. A gate keeper or watchman would live nearby until the time when the Turnpike Trust had toll cottages and gates built. In 1789 a dispute was brought to the notice of the Distington Court Leet Meeting where fourteen Jurors attended which confirms the fact that there was a gate or gates into the village of Distington.

*'Regarding a dispute arisen between Peter Peele of Distington Gentleman and James Hall of Whitehaven to the right of a said James Hall to hang a gate in the road which leads from Distington to the house of Peter Peele at Prospect Hill. It was declared that the said James Hall has a right to hang a gate there. But for as much as we apprehend that the want of a gate cannot be attended with any inconvenience or damage to the said James Hall so long as the gate leading out of Distington Town at the head of the aforesaid road is upheld and kept in repair. We recommend that James Hall not to hang a gate at the West side of his said field so long as the said gate of the said road is well and sufficiently repaired an upheld and said parties have likewise the consideration of making the wall of the south side of the said road from the head of the road at Distington to the bridge leading into the said field called Whitterdale and repair of wall in the future and making and repairing the said road'.*

*Distington Toll Cottage, circa 1890,*
*by kind permission of Mike Pritt, Distington*

In 1811 the stagecoaches travelled through this hamlet. Houses, cottages and farms were scattered along a mile or so of the road and the surrounding countryside was considered rather wild at this time. There were several inns in the village along the main street. In 1815 Robert Bell was the innkeeper of the Globe Hotel thought to have been the main coaching inn. He was also the local builder and his mother Margaret kept the house and his sister also Margaret was a barmaid. Court Leet meetings and social occasions where held here along with local sales. The Black Lion a late 1700's inn now a private house, the Boot Inn another very old establishment situated at the south of the village was recorded in 1814 as 'to let', *'To be let by private contract that well accommodated and ancient public house called Bridge End, Distington and also known by the sign of The Boot'.* This inn has now been a residential property for some time.

The 'Royal Sailor' was not scheduled to make a stop, however the coachman probably did pick up and drop passengers if there was room and if there was mail to drop off. A lame horse would also be changed, as the road ahead to Whitehaven, became quite hilly.

*The Globe Hotel, Distington, circa 1905, by kind permission of Carlisle Library*

To the south of Distington in the latter years of the stagecoach era the Cumberland Museum created by J.R.Wallace was opened. Those who would find it of interest may have travelled out from Whitehaven, Workington or Cockermouth in a hired Gig, or Wagonette that seated about six for the day. The vast collection of specimens from around the world housed in an unusually designed house made an attractive visit.

Leaving Distington the stagecoach made its way south towards Moresby. For the passengers who sat on top of the coach the ruins of Hayes Castle would have come into view. The Lakeland fells could also be seen on a fine day. Moresby village consisted of just a few cottages, the village expanded later when villas and some better farmhouses were built. Ahead the coastline and the sea can also be seen. Along a side road to Parton once a small seaport now just a fishing village, stands Moresby Hall the ancestral seat of the Moricebys and the Fletcher family's. Opposite commanding good views all round is the site of the old Roman Fort of Gabrosentum.

With the rough road rising up and down for these last few miles, the coachman would be working hard to contain the horses. Knowing that Bransty Brow was the last hill before descending down into Whitehaven, it would take all his efforts and the strength of the horses to get his passengers safely to their destination. Early stagecoaches did not have brakes!

Long Bransty Gate the last tollgate on the route lay ahead at the junction to the seaside village of Parton. This toll gate was also known locally as the 'old pay house' it was demolished in the middle of the 1800's for the new road which wound its way around Bransty Hill and descended more gradually into Whitehaven as shown on John Woods map of 1832. A new toll gate cottage was built further along the road in 1854 at the base of Bransty Hill. The date is over the front door and the present owner keeps it in good order. The old turnpike gate post and hinges is incorporated in the front wall.

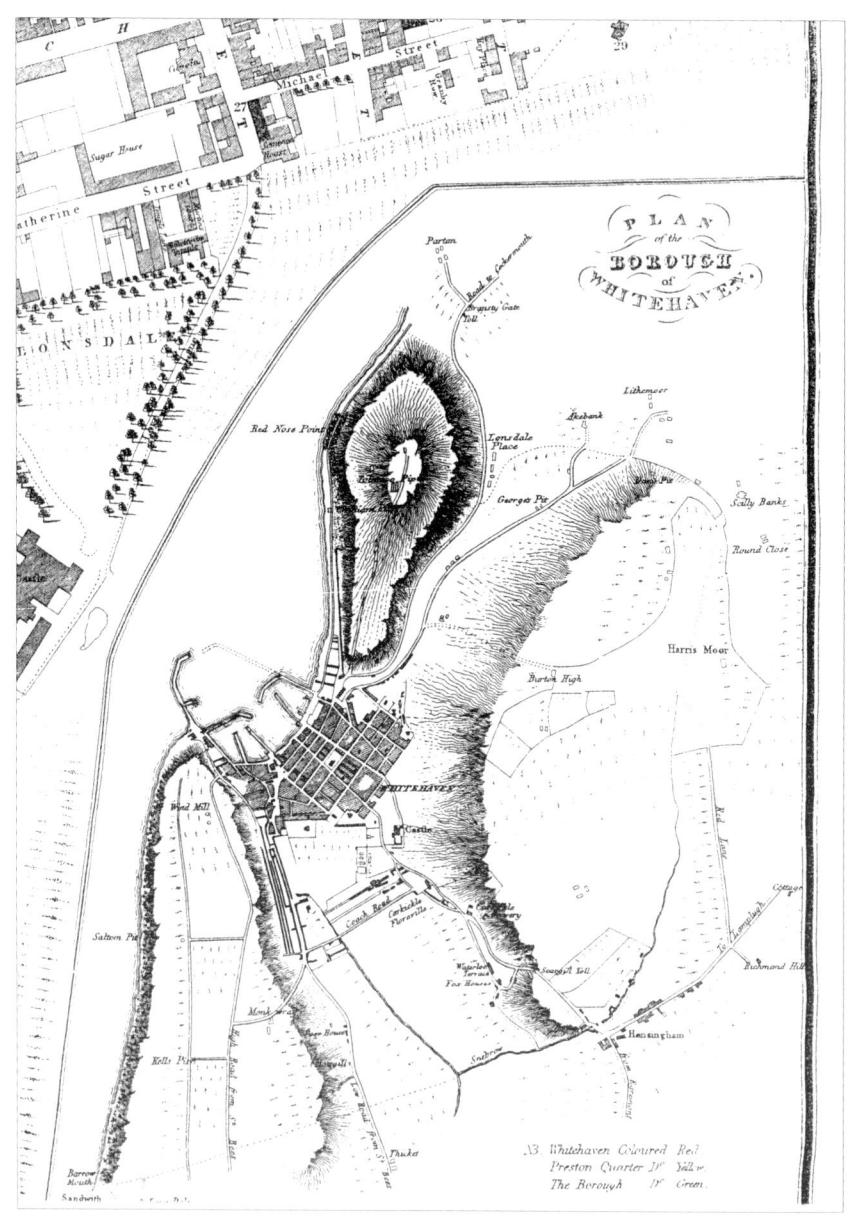

*John Woods Map, 1832, by kind permission of the Carlisle Record Office*

86

In 1811 the stagecoach took the steep ascent up the Brow and down into Whitehaven. It was a long pull for the horses, with the weight of the coach, passengers and luggage they strained every muscle to climb the hill. On some steep inclines passengers had to alight and walk to the top of the hill, before re-boarding the coach and resuming their journey. The horses used regularly on this route would know that they were not far from the end of their journey, where stables and a feed were waiting.

Arriving at the top of the Brow a good coachman would ease the pressure off the horses and let them have a blow while the passengers who had alighted had time to regain their seats. From this high point the passengers had marvellous views of the coastline and on a fine day could see the hills of the Isle of Man.

Situated along the top of Bransty Brow the coach passed the furnaces and tobacco pipes where the condemned, damaged or contraband tobacco was burnt. Originally this process was carried out behind the Customs House in Whitehaven until the local inhabitants complained of the smell. An Act passed in 1744 enabled Mr Peter How one of the main tobacco importers to build new furnaces on the hill outside the town. The tall chimneys that took the smoke away into the atmosphere could be seen for miles around. They were finally demolished in 1923.

Smuggling still continued along this coast well into the 1800's but not in such force as in the 1700's when it was rife. It became more difficult to smuggle with Revenue boats patrolling the waters and the Riding Officers patrolling the beaches and cliffs. The odd boat or two was seized carrying spirits, tea and tobacco from the Isle of Man trying to land along the Whitehaven coast and under the Bransty cliffs.

After passing the Tobacco furnaces at the top of Bransty Brow the coach made its way towards the hill down into Whitehaven. Here

*Tobacco Pipes, Bransty, Whitehaven*

the passengers could see the town spread out below embraced by the green hills with the harbour full of ships. The town was planned and laid out in a formal fashion by Sir John Lowther in the late seventeenth century. With the coal and tobacco trade increasing, the population and the town grew considerably larger over the following century. On a fine day what a scene this must have been.

As the road descended steeply the coachman trusting his horses to keep a steady pace they made their way slowly down the hill. In later times coaches had brakes, but were not thought to be very efficient. When the coach going down hill was tilted forward it tightened a leather strap around the rear wheel hub. Sometimes the guard would get down and walk along with a shoe (not his own) as it was called, ready to put under the wheel if the descent got difficult. The passengers may have taken a safer option and walked down enjoying the scenery on the way.

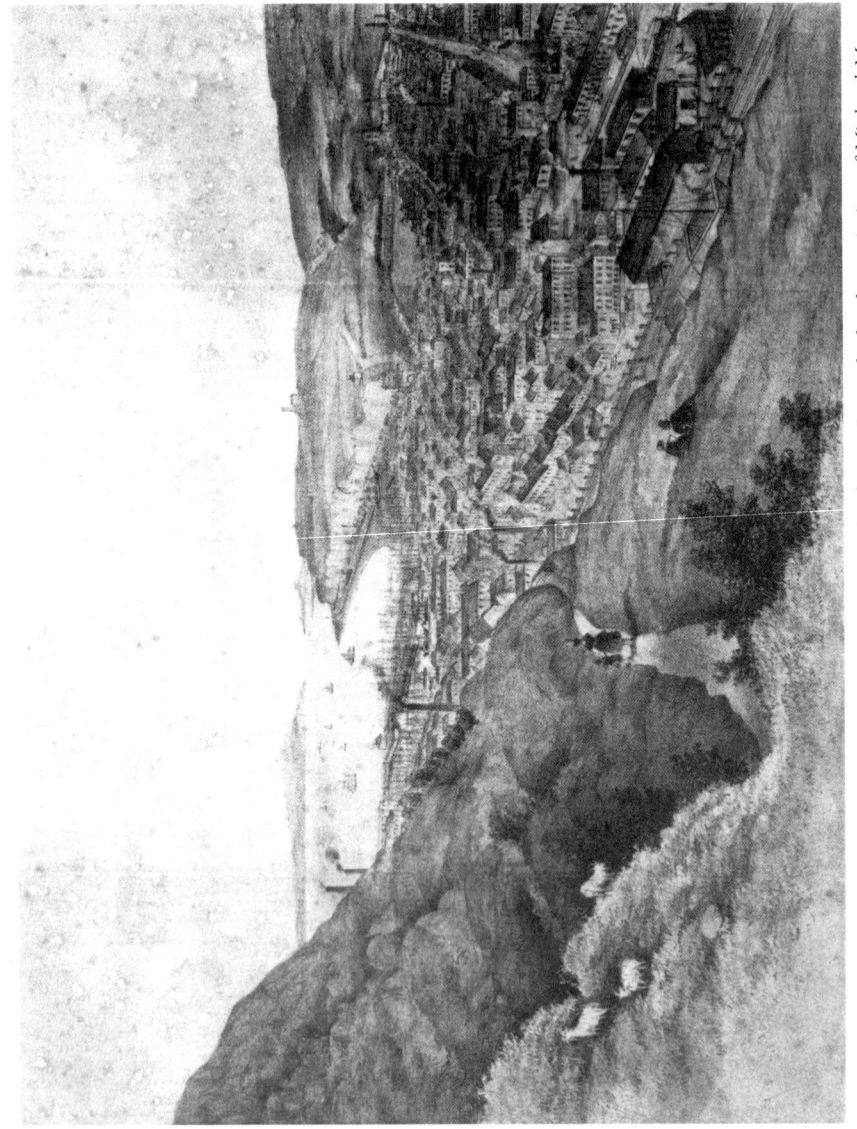

*Old print of Whitehaven looking towards Bransty and the old Tobacco Pipes, by kind permission of Michael Moon*

## Chapter Six

## ARRIVING IN WHITEHAVEN

Arriving at the bottom of the hill from Bransty or in later years the new turnpike road which went around the east side of Bransty hill the stagecoach made its way into the bustling and busy town of Whitehaven. As recorded by earlier travellers the town was found to be dirty and noisy, with the sound of shipwrights and the various workmen in the factories around the harbour going about their daily work. The furnaces, coal pits in the area and the wagons that conveyed the coal over Bransty Arch to the holds of the waiting vessels along the quay side filled the air with coal dust and smoke, as well as the dirt off the roads kicked up by the passing traffic. Passengers on the coach after seeing the wonder of the fair town from above at Bransty hill would be surprised at what they had descended into as they made their way through the crowded streets especially on market days. In winter time the passengers arriving in the evening found the streets lit by oil lamps making it very murky. On exploring further several respectable streets with fine houses

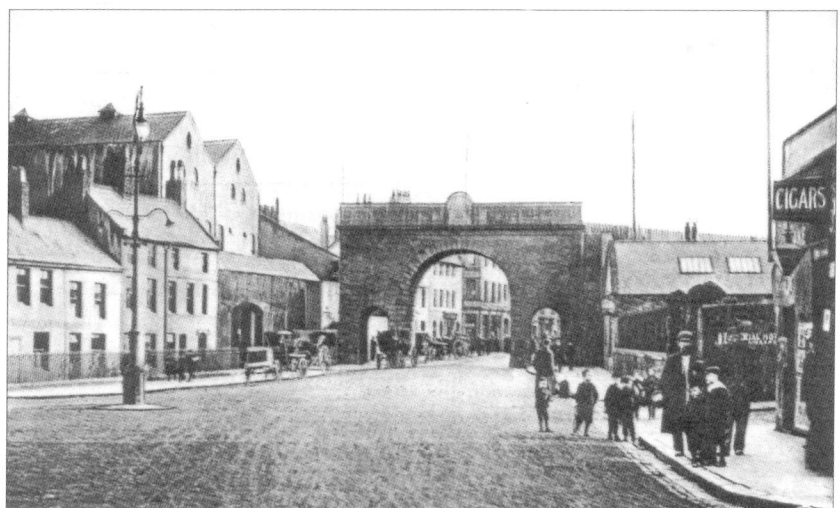

*Bramsty Arch, Whitehaven Built 1803, from the Beacon Collection*

enhanced the town including the palatial residence of the Earl of Lonsdale. After 1806 an Act was passed for many of the streets to be paved and the housing of a night watchman. The new Earl of Lonsdale, Sir William Lowther a generous man rebuilt Lowther Hall which had been destroyed by fire in the previous generation and now known as Lowther Castle. He did much to improve the town using his high status to advantage, which would have been seen during the stagecoach era.

The stagecoach continued along to the Globe Inn which is situated on the corner of King Street named after Charles II who granted lands to Sir John Lowther and Duke Street another royal connection with James II when Duke of York. Weary passengers would alight, pleased to have arrived at their destination. Some would be met by light carriages or gigs to be taken on further. Others would make their way into the inn to be met by the proprietor where his generous hospitality would be gratefully accepted after a very tiring journey especially for those who had travelled all the way from Carlisle.

*Stage Coach travelling, circa 1828, by kind permission of Carlisle Library*

*Duke Street, Whitehaven.*

*The Globe Hotel, Duke Street, from the Beacon Museum Collection*

*The Black Lion Inn, from the Beacon Museum Collection*

The Globe Inn was a substantial building with three floors, cellars and stabling for guests horses and carriages. In more recent times it was known as the Globe Hotel. Like many of the other prominent inns in towns it had a very good social life with dinners, meetings and various social functions held on its premises. Duke Street residents consisted of many ships Captains, mariners, the usual shop keepers and traders and there were several other inns.

In July 1820 the Globe Inn was advertised to let and was at that time occupied by Mr John Mounsey. Having not been able to re-let the Inn a further advertisement three years later in December 1823 shows:

*THE GLOBE INN, WHITEHAVEN,*
*JOHN MOUNSEY*
*Deeply impressed with Gratitude for the numerous Favours, which during a period of Forty Years he has as an Innkeeper, respectfully announces that he has transferred his business to his Daughter, in whose behalf he presumes to solicit a Continuance of the Public Favour.*

ISABELLA MOUNSEY
*Most respectfully informs the Public and Travellers in general, that she has recently entered on the above Inn, where she has laid in an excellent and extensive Stock of Spirits, Wines &c, &c, and fitted up the Apartments with Beds and other Furniture in the newest Style; and begs to assure those who may honour the House with their Countenance and Support, that no exertion shall be wanting on her part, to promote their Accommodation and Comfort.*
*Whitehaven, December 1st 1823.*

The Black Lion Inn in King Street was also a coaching inn, and in March 1812 it changed hands when a Mr Hale became the proprietor. He states in an advertisement that:

*'John Hale respectfully requests gentleman travellers and the public in general that he has now opened the Black Lion Inn situated in King Street and Strand Street, Whitehaven. Where his constant endeavours will be used to give the upmost satisfaction to all those who may be pleased to favour him with their commands. No expense will be spared for the accommodation of gentleman travellers. Most excellent stabling and convenience for carriages with steady careful ostlers. N.B. Neat Post Chaises and careful drivers."*

By May 1814 after two years we find Mr John Hale no longer the innkeeper of the Black Lion as the following advertisement shows:

*'THOMAS JACKSON late waiter of the Kings Arms, Kendal respectively informs Commercial Gentleman travellers and the Public in General that he has taken the large and commodious Inn known by the sign of the BLACK LION situated in King Street and Strand Street. Whitehaven.*
*The house is at present undergoing considerable alterations as well as a thorough repair and will be opened in a few days when Thomas Jackson hopes that the accommodations of every kind will be found agreeable to all who please to honour him with their commands – which it will be his endeavour to merit, on all occasions by the strictest attention to the duties of his station.*
*Besides the centre situation of the Black Lion it possesses every appendant convenience of an Inn, in excellent Stabling, carriage stands, etc, etc.*
*Whitehaven 28ᵗʰ May 1814'*

By 1829 the 'Royal Sailor' used the Black Lion Inn as their final stop on the route. Not a very impressive frontage to the inn, but quite spacious inside with many bedrooms and function rooms. The stables and coach house were situated at the rear in Strand Street. Mr Thomas Jackson was still the innkeeper. Many businessmen, merchants and salesmen met at this inn to carry out their business. Sales of property and ships and various functions were also held here. King Street was noted for respectable residences along its street, housing the various merchants of the day with their warehouses at the rear on East Strand.

Whitehaven was always a very busy bustling town and port, with much activity going on in the harbour. Ships unloading their cargos, coal wagons arriving from the pit heads to be loaded and shipped to Ireland and other ports. The shipbuilding, various manufactories, trades and mills that were situated around this area all went towards creating a very busy and prosperous scene.

The upkeep of roads into Whitehaven was very important, as the amount of traffic that used them soon wore the surfaces away. The new turnpike road that was built in the late 1820's around Bransty Brow into the town was a much needed asset.

The 'Defiance' stagecoach from Penrith and the 'Royal Mail' from Kendal travelling via Keswick, Cockermouth and Workington used this new road to bring many passengers and the mail. These passengers may have travelled from London, Edinburgh or other parts of the country the day before. Some may have chosen to spend the night in a local inn or hostelry before continuing the next day to other parts of Cumberland.

Another means of conveyance from Carlisle to Whitehaven was a Gig. This was advertised in 1820 by:

*JAMES MARINER*
*'Respectfully begs leave to inform the Public that he has*
*commenced*
*RUNNING A GIG*
*Between Carlisle and Whitehaven*
*And hopes, by Punctuality and Care, to merit the Patronage of the*

*Public.*

*The Gig will leave Mr Snowden's Blue Bell Inn, Scotch Street, Carlisle, every Monday, Wednesday, and Friday Morning at Eight o'Clock through Wigton, Allonby, Maryport, Workington and will arrive in Whitehaven the same Evening at Seven o'Clock, at Mr Bird's Golden Lion, Market Place; whence it will Start every Tuesday, Thursday, and Saturday Morning at Seven o'Clock for Carlisle by the same route.*

*N.B. – At the earnest request of many of his Friends, J.M. Intends to run his GIG every Sunday in future.*

*The Gig will stop at Mr.Barns, Black Swan, Wigton; Mr Stamper Armstrongs, Brown Cow, Maryport; and the other usual Places of call on the Road.*

*J.M. will not be answerable for any Parcel above the Value of £5, unless Entered and Paid for accordingly.'*

*Whitehaven June 19, 1820.*


Gigs were two wheeled vehicles built fairly high and used quite often by commercial travellers. Holding a driver and two other people it proved a rather expensive way of getting around the country. It had a boot at the back for luggage and a hood that was raised in bad weather. Not much protection from the oncoming elements at the front. James Mariner must have changed his horse and stopped for refreshments during the journey of eleven hours. Not a journey for the faint hearted on such a lightweight means of transport.

*Maryport Railway Station, circa 1841, taken from the Account of the Maryport & Carlisle Railway 1909, by kind permission of Carlisle Library*

## Chapter Seven

## THE END OF A STAGECOACH ERA

By 1843 the railways were arriving on the scene, people were getting excited at the prospect of being swept along by these giant machines issuing out volumes of smoke as they puffed along the tracks. It would mean that passengers could get there and back in a day from most main towns on Carlisle and Whitehaven route. This spelt out doom for the stagecoach companies and proprietors. They battled on while the various sections of the railway were built but inevitably they had to give way to this new technology.

*The first timetable issued by the Maryport & Carlisle Railway, by kind permission of Carlisle Library*

The first part of the railway line was built from Maryport to Aspatria via the Arkleby Pits by April 1841 to enable the coal to be transported

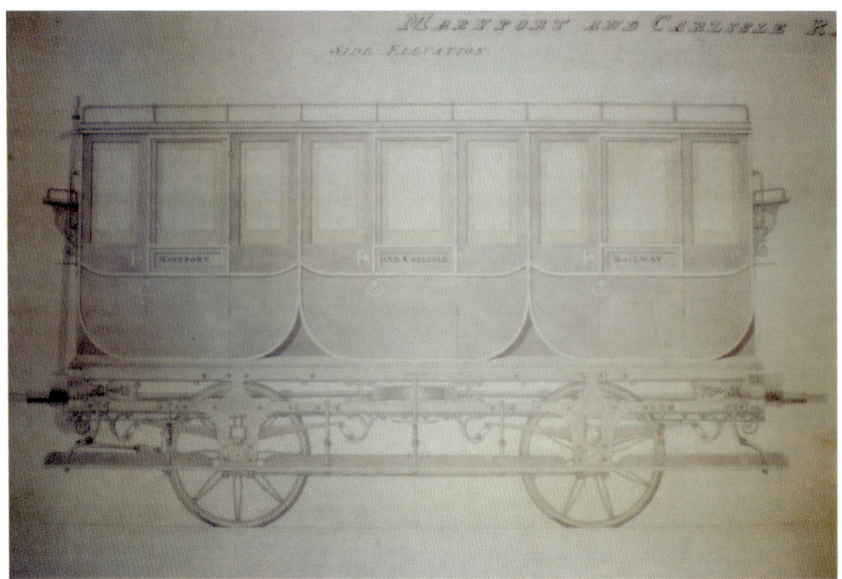

*1st Class coach, Carlisle and Maryport Railway, by kind permission of Carlisle Library*

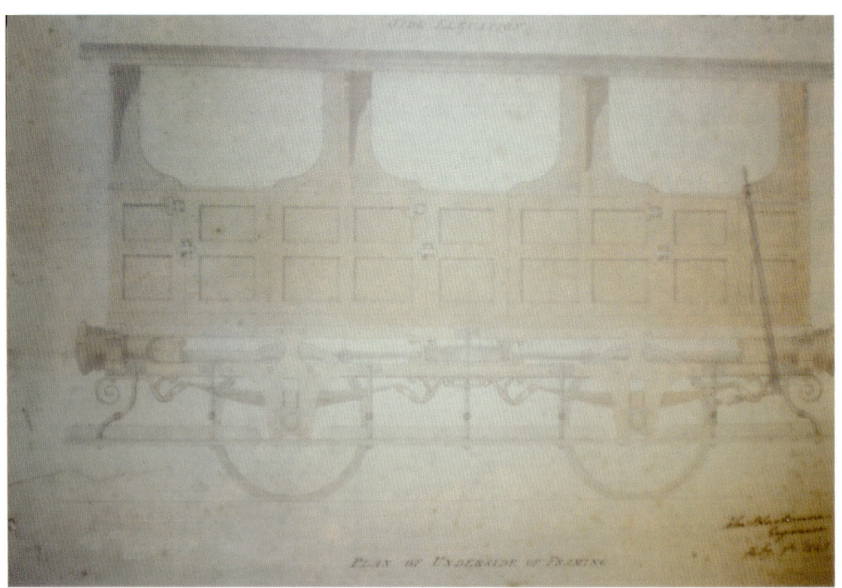

*2nd Class coach, Carlisle and Maryport Railway, by kind permission of Carlisle Library*

quicker to the port. The line from Carlisle to Wigton was then built and commenced service on 3rd May 1843. The next section from Wigton to Aspatria by February 1845 and finally the line was completed through to Whitehaven by 1847. This part of the railway line from Maryport to Whitehaven was considered to be the most scenic of the route running close to the sea. Passengers enjoyed fine views of the Solway coast.

While these sections of the new railway where being built the Railway Companies offered a convenient coach travel to enable passengers to get to their destinations.

On the 3rd May 1842 an advertisement was issued by the Maryport and Carlisle Railway in the Cumberland Pacquet offering the following services:

*'Travelling between Whitehaven and Carlisle by the cheapest and swiftest coaches and on or after the 10th May the 'Safety Coach' will leave the Black Lion and Globe Inns, Whitehaven at 9.30 in the*

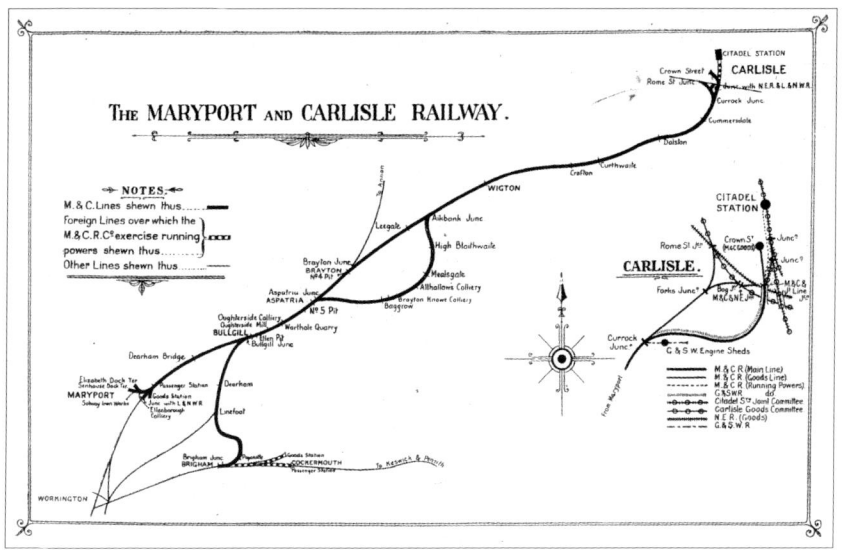

*Maryport & Carlisle Railway, taken from the Account of the Maryport & Carlisle Railway 1909, by kind permission of Carlisle Library*

*morning daily (except Sundays) and reach the Royal Hotel, Carlisle at 2.30 aforenoon. The Engineer Coach' will leave the Royal Hotel, Carlisle at 9.30 am. and reach the Black Lion and Globe Inns at 2.30.pm. Performed by Messrs Croall & Henderson of Carlisle and Robert Fearon of Maryport after their best manner'.*

On the 10th May 1843 the Maryport and Carlisle Railway Company were still offering a service by the 'Engineer Coach' to convey passengers in four hours, twice daily from Carlisle to Whitehaven via Aspatria. Leaving at 9.45 in the morning and 3.45 in the afternoon arriving at 1.45 and 7.45 respectively. The fares between Carlisle and Wigton were First Class 2s and Second Class 1s.6d. Another coach called the 'Railway Coach' commenced running on the 5th June 1843 also in connexion with the railways. It left Whitehaven twice daily. The 9.15 morning coach arrived in Carlisle in time to connect with the Newcastle train enabling passengers to complete their journey by coach and train the same day. The coach fares between Carlisle and Whitehaven were Inside and 1st Class 7s.6d and Outside and 2nd Class 5s.0d., and no fees to the coachman or guard. This speedy service was no mean feat for the horses.

The journey appears to be quite expensive for passengers travelling by coach and rail from Whitehaven through to Newcastle. Only the 'well to do', merchants and businessmen could afford to travel by this means.

*by kind permission of Carlisle Library*

Innkeepers and hoteliers in the various towns would view the coming railway as profit making with the increase of travellers and tourists to the area. The Globe Inn in Whitehaven was advertised for sale on 20th July 1847 as an enterprising proposition within walking distance to the railway station.

*'The very valuable and eligible Premises, situate at the Head of King Street and Corner of Duke Street and Strand Street, in the Town of Whitehaven aforesaid known by the Name of*

## *'THE GLOBE INN'*

*Recently tenanted by Mrs Mc.Kinley, deceased, and at present unoccupied.*

*Having Three large Frontages to King Street, Duke Street, and Strand Street. The Front to King Street comprises Forty-six Feet Six Inches; to Duke Street, facing directly up Tangier Street, Seventy-five Feet Two Inches; and to Strand Street (to which, from King Street, it extends direct through) Forty-seven Feet Two inches, or thereabouts. The Accommodation consists of Six good Sitting Rooms, with Bar and Bar Parlour, Nine Roomy Sleeping Apartments, commodious Kitchen and Offices, with Four Servants Bed Rooms above; good Attics over the whole; Larder, Pantry, Ale, Wine, and other Cellars; large Yard, with a Twelve-stalled Stable, and Hay Loft above.*

*On the death of the late Tenant innumerable Applications were made by parties wishing to become Tenants of these Premises, at very high Rents, but the Trustees considered it better to dispose of the Inn, with immediate Possession to a Purchaser, rather than to impress any Conditions with respect to the time of its Occupation. The intended Terminus and Station of the Whitehaven and Carlisle Railway, now forming, will be within One Hundred Yards from this Lot, and a Situation more admirably adapted for an extensive Hotel and Posting-house, in Connexion with the Railway, and for the general Convenience of the Public, is not to be met with in the Town, combining as it does centrality of Situation, and easy access to the Harbour, Public Offices, Piers, Places of Business and Amusement and commanding from Duke Street a good View of the Harbour and Offing. Should this Lot fall into the Hands of any spirited and enterprising Individual, it would command a very large Proportion of first-rate Business'.*

John Fearon became the proprietor of the Globe Hotel and ran it for several years until John Moat followed him in 1861 with further renovations to the premises as his advertisement shows with the added attraction of a 'taxi' service to and from the station by omnibus. By this time most hotels ran their own private omnibuses, they carried four or more people to various functions in the town and the railway station.

*by kind permission of Carlisle Library*

The omnibus also known as a 'horse bus' was first designed by George Shillibeer in France he later brought his design to London and it was used on the roads from 1829 to carry eighteen or more passengers. Eventually these larger coaches pulled by three or four horses were used to ferry tourists around the Lake District.

Other smaller coaching businesses tried to fill the gap like Mr Jas. Brindle of the Queens Head Inn, Wigton. He commenced running the 'Victoria Coach' from 5th June 1843 from Keswick to Carlisle via Wigton enabling passengers to connect with the train to Newcastle. He announced in the Carlisle Journal:

*"Mr Brindle returns thanks to his Friends and the Public generally, for the support given to the Victoria Coach, and begs to inform them that on Monday, the 5th of June inst., he will commence RUNNING the VICTORIA, DAILY, from KESWICK TO CARLISLE, and back the same Day. – The Coach will leave Keswick at Seven every morning, Cockermouth at Half-past Eight, Cockbridge at Ten, where Twenty Minutes will be allowed for Breakfast, Wigton Half-past Eleven, and reach Carlisle in time for the Mid-day Train*

*to Newcastle. She will return by the same route to Keswick, leaving Carlisle at Two P.M., and arriving in Keswick at Eight o'clock in the Evening".*

But this was short lived. He states in a further advertisement dated September 14th 1843 that this service would cease due to "*heavy tolls and the numerous other conveyances on the road*".

| REDUCED FARES by the WHITEHAVEN & CARLISLE ROYAL MAIL COACH. | | | | | | | | | | |
|---|---|---|---|---|---|---|---|---|---|---|
| FROM | TO WORKINGTON | | TO MARYPORT | | TO ALLONBY | | TO WIGTON | | TO CARLISLE | |
| | Inside | Outside | Inside | Outside | Inside | Outside | Inside | Outside | Inside | Outside |
| | s. D. | s. D. | s. D. | s. D. | s. D. | s. D. | s. D. | s. D. | s. D. | s. D. |
| Whitehaven | 1 6 | 1 0 | 3 0 | 2 0 | 5 0 | 3 0 | 7 0 | 4 6 | 8 0 | 5 0 |
| Workington | | | 1 6 | 1 0 | 3 0 | 2 0 | 5 0 | 3 0 | 7 0 | 4 6 |
| Maryport | 1 6 | 1 0 | | | 1 6 | 1 0 | 3 0 | 2 0 | 5 0 | 4 0 |
| Allonby | 3 0 | 2 0 | 1 6 | 1 0 | | | 3 0 | 2 0 | 5 0 | 4 0 |
| Wigton | 5 0 | 3 0 | 3 0 | 2 0 | 3 0 | 2 0 | | | 2 6 | 1 6 |

Short distances charged proportionably low. JAMES FITZSIMONS, Manager.

*The Maryport Locomotive & Monthly Advertiser, Jan 6th 1843,*
*by kind permission of Carlisle Record Office*

Instead he would just run the coach between Wigton and Keswick. Picking up or leaving passengers at the railway station in Wigton in time for the arrival of the train to and from Carlisle. He also adds that "*In consequence of this alteration Mr Brindle will have a number of well seasoned HORSES to dispose of*".

As the stage coach business declined many horses became surplus to requirements. Some where sold on and adapted for saddle and harness. Others were bought and used for farming purposes.

Coach drivers and guards who drove the different sections of the route found them selves without work and would have to look to other alternatives. In 1862 it was noted in the Carlisle Journal the death of a stagecoach driver. '*At his residence James Terrace, Botchergate, on the 9th inst, Mr John Irving, for many years driver of the Royal Sailor Coach between Carlisle and Wigton, in the 68th year of his age,- deeply regretted by a large circle of friends*'. One wonders what he may have turned his hand to in the last twenty years of his life.

Coach drivers and guards who drove the different sections of the route with this new form of travel by rail the stagecoach companies decided to reduce their fares to encourage passengers to continue using their mode of transport. One such advertisement was found in the Maryport Locomotive and Monthly Advertiser dated January 6th 1843.

But it was a losing battle and many businesses went under, including the many trades that kept the stagecoaches and horses on the road. The blacksmith was able to continue his work as he was much needed for the various mechanical repairs around the villages and farms, along with shoeing cart horses and the local gentries' carriage and riding horses.

As stagecoaches ceased to use the various routes, many wayside coaching inns found it difficult to keep their businesses open with just the local trade. By the turn of the century many had closed turning their premises into private houses or moving on. Staff had to look elsewhere for work or learn a new trade. This was hard for people who did not like change and rued the day that the railways had come to stay.

During this time of change various acts of parliament were brought out regarding the railways and stagecoach travel on the roads. Because of the new railway system cutting across the countryside, many new bridges were built. These had to be of the right dimensions to enable stagecoaches to go over or under as the case may be. '*The open space of the arch to be constructed of not less than eighteen feet in height, and the descent under a bridge or over not to extend one foot in thirty feet. Also screens or fences to be erected where the railway runs along the side of the roads so as not to endanger or frighten travellers and horses'.*

By 1850 coach travel had almost ceased in the area. Some coach companies looked to the tourist trade and advertised visits to the Lake District. Designing larger coaches holding more passengers they could transport larger groups around the countryside. But even this failed as motorised vehicles took to the roads.

It was stated in the Maryport Locomotive and Monthly Advertiser of April 1842 in a letter to the editor. That a new monthly paper was being issued by the name of the *Royal Sailor*, and this being in rather bad taste as the old stagecoach of the same name had only just the previous week been driven off the road by the Maryport and Carlisle Railway Company.

This old stagecoach service had served for 31 years through all weathers and the bad road conditions of the day getting its passengers to their destinations safely. With only one known accident recorded along this route near Thursby in 1829 and no other mishaps or wayside hold ups by highwaymen it truly is a record of the courage of the fine coachmen and guards that served the route and not forgetting the strong stout hearted horses that pulled these coaches.

# BIBLIOGRAPHY

| | |
|---|---|
| Bailey, J.B. | Ancient & Modern 1883 |
| Blake, J & B. | The Story of Carlisle 1958 |
| Bradbury, D. | Parton 2000 |
| Burgess, John | The Victorian Heritage of Cumbria |
| Burton, A & P. | The Green Bag Travellers 1978 |
| Byres R.L.M. | History of Workington |
| Callender & Dixon. | Moresby Hall & its Owners in the Olden Times 1875 |

Carlisle Journal
Cumberland Pacquet

| | |
|---|---|
| Davis P. & Mail B. | First Post – From Penny Black to Present Day 1990 |

Directory & Gazetteer of Cumberland 1861

| | |
|---|---|
| Eaglesham Nancy | Whitehaven and the Tobacco Trade 1979 |
| Fancy, H. | Whitehaven 1996 |
| Harper C.G. | The Manchester & Glasgow Road 1907 |
| Hay, Daniel | Whitehaven an Illustrated History 1966 |
| Haining Peter, | The English Highwayman 1991 |
| Hindle, B.P. | Road & Trackways – The Lake District |
| Hughes Edward | North County Life in the Eighteenth Century Vol. II. Cumb. & West. 1700 -1830 |
| Jackson H. & M. | West Cumbrian Coast. History of the Maryport & Carlisle Railway. |
| Jackson W. | Whitehaven 1878 |
| Jollies | Cumberland Guide & Directory 1811 |

Maryport Locomotive & Monthly Advertiser 1842- 4

| | |
|---|---|
| Magna Britannia | 1816 |
| Mee Arthur. | The Lake Counties 1937 |
| Mountfield, D. | Stage & Mail Coaches 2003 |
| Parson & Whites | History, Directory & Gazetteer of Cumberland & Westmorland 1829 |
| Pigots Directory | 1834 |
| Routledge,A.W. | History & Guide of Whitehaven 2002 |
| Railway Magazines | No 148, 1909,  & No 535, 1942 |
| Senhouse, H. | Papers 1790 |
| The Citizen | Fortnightly Periodical 1822 - 1830 |
| Thompson, Keith. | Images of England – Maryport 2000 |
| Trevelyan G.M. | English Social History 1942 |
| Watney Marylian | The Elegant Carriage |

Whitehaven Gazette

| | |
|---|---|
| Williams, L.A. | Road Transport in Cumbria in the 19th Century.1975 |
| Wright, G.N. | Turnpike Roads 1997 |
| Various Transactions | C.W.A.S. |
| Yarwood Doreen | Outline of English Costume 1967 |